CW01033245

Psychological Warfare

*The Ultimate Guide to Understanding
Human Behavior, Brainwashing,
Propaganda, Deception, Negotiation, Dark
Psychology, and Manipulation*

Contents

INTRODUCTION 1

CHAPTER 1: WHAT IS PSYCHOLOGICAL WARFARE? 2

SIMPLE FORMS OF PSYOP.. 3

TYPICAL TACTICS OF PSYOP 4

EARLY EXAMPLES OF PSYCHOLOGICAL WARFARE................................... 5

MODERN USE OF PSYCHOLOGICAL WARFARE 6

PSYOPS IN EVERYDAY LIFE... 9

CHAPTER 2: IT ALL STARTS WITH DARK PERSONALITIES 11

THREE PERSONALITY TRAITS 11

THE "D" FACTORS 16

HOW ARE DARK TRIAD TRAITS MEASURED?... 17

CHAPTER 3: THE ART OF DECEPTION..20

HOW TO RECOGNIZE AN EFFECTIVE LIAR 20

THE BODY LANGUAGE OF A LIAR... 22

WHAT ARE THE DIFFERENT TYPES OF DECEPTION?.............................. 25

CHAPTER 4: PSYCHOLOGICAL WARFARE IN RELATIONSHIPS 32

WHAT ARE GASLIGHTING TACTICS? 32

THE KEY SIGNS TO LOOK FOR TO IDENTIFY AN UNHEALTHY USE OF SILENCE 38

CHAPTER 5: PSYCHOLOGICAL WARFARE AT WORK 40

How to Detect Dark Personality Traits.. 41

Workplace Bullying 42

Classic Signs that Bullying is Occurring in the Workplace............ 43

What to Do if You Recognize that Bullying is Happening in Your Workplace 47

Here Are Some Great Tips to Help You Prevent Bullying in the Workplace 47

CHAPTER 6: PROPAGANDA I: POLITICAL PROPAGANDA 49

Here Are Some of the Ways the Soviet Union Disseminated Propaganda.. 49

Propaganda in Nazi Germany 51

Political Propaganda in the US.. 53

CHAPTER 7: PROPAGANDA II: THE MANIPULATIVE MEDIA................57

Some Strategies That the Mass Media Employs................................ 58

Propaganda in Advertising 61

CHAPTER 8: MIND CONTROL AND BRAINWASHING 65

Who Would Be Interested in Brainwashing?...................................... 66

Manipulation Techniques.. 67

Mind Control in the Drug Industry.. 69

Operation Midnight Climax... 71

CHAPTER 9: HOW CULTS WORK 73

Common Misconceptions About Cults... 75

Should We Be Afraid of Cults?.. 77

Extreme and Disturbing Cult Movements in Recent History 78

CHAPTER 10: NLP AND DARK NEGOTIATION TECHNIQUES..............82

What is NLP? 82

Are You Being Subjected to NLP Techniques?................................... 83

Signs That NLP is Being Used 83

Dark Negotiation Techniques 84

Become Better at Negotiating 85

How to Deal with These Tactics... 86

OTHER NLP METHODS... 87

CHAPTER 11: CYBERCRIMINALS 90

WHAT IS CYBERCRIME?.. 91

COMMON FORMS OF CYBERCRIME... 92

PROTECT YOURSELF AGAINST CYBERCRIMINALS 94

CHAPTER 12: PROTECTING YOURSELF 97

CHOOSE YOUR NEWS SOURCE CAREFULLY 98

RELIABLE SOURCES THAT PRODUCE QUALITY JOURNALISM............ 98

WAYS TO CLEAR YOUR MIND AND THINK FOR YOURSELF............... 100

HOW TO AVOID BEING MANIPULATED IN RELATIONSHIPS............... 101

HOW TO AVOID MANIPULATION IN GENERAL 102

CONCLUSION 107

HERE'S ANOTHER BOOK BY NEIL MORTON THAT YOU MIGHT LIKE...108

REFERENCES 109

Introduction

Does psychological warfare sound like something out of a James Bond novel? It could never affect you, could it? The truth is we all encounter some form of psychological warfare daily. This book is packed with easy to understand, jargon free ways to recognize the people who are trying to mess with your mind. If you want a comprehensive guide to stop being manipulated by the media, by your boss, or even by your partner, then look no further.

Expert advice doesn't have to be complicated and difficult to understand. *Psychological Warfare: The Ultimate Guide to Understanding Human Behavior, Brainwashing, Propaganda, Deception, Negotiation, Dark Psychology, and Manipulation* contains methods and exercises for everyone. Even if you are unaware of any form of manipulation or deception around you, it is worth knowing what potential dangers may arise in the future.

Chapter 1: What is Psychological Warfare?

Psychological warfare is known by a variety of names: PSYWAR, political warfare, "Hearts and Minds," PSYOP, and propaganda, to name a few. While most people are aware of the emergence of PSYWAR in the Second World War, it has much older origins and can be traced back as far as mankind itself.

Psychological warfare is the use of non-combat techniques to mislead and intimidate opponents and influence their psychological makeup. The techniques employed are designed to target thoughts, emotions, and attitudes with propaganda and threats to influence a person's actions.

Propaganda is not a threatening concept when used alone. Daniel Lerner wrote about the theory of "black," "white," and "gray" propaganda in his 1949 book *Sykewar; Psychological Warfare Against Germany, D-Day to V-E Day.*

• **White propaganda:** this defines the use of truthful information with a moderate bias to influence opponents. In the Second World War, this included millions of leaflets being dropped from planes over friendly and enemy territory. The leaflets stated their source and contained information designed to encourage support and contributions from the target audience.

- **Gray propaganda:** this will often be anonymous and contain information that is mainly true. If there are untrue statements, it is unlikely that they can be disproven. It involves presenting legitimate arguments that are free from agenda but have undefined sources.

- **Black propaganda:** put simply, fake news. This type of propaganda can contain both true and false statements, but it will appear to be legitimately sourced. This type of propaganda is designed to be wholly believable and is distributed with the intent of subversion.

The difference between gray and black propaganda is often a fine line. The most effective form of black propaganda is formed to look like it has come from trusted sources. Often the biggest giveaway is any links to gray propaganda that are less convincing.

There are many different forms of psychological warfare, but the result is just the same. The tactics employed are designed to demoralize, influence beliefs, change motives, and stir emotions. The targets of these tactics can range from the man on the street to the highest form of government, with everyone in between included.

Simple Forms of PSYOP

- **Word of mouth:** face to face communication may seem to be trustworthy, but it can be affected by rumors and mistruths.

- **Entertainment media sources:** we may feel that television and film are purely used for entertainment, but we can be influenced by them without knowing. Subtle messages and information can be presented in a way that seems like harmless fun, but it can be an effective way of altering people's thoughts and beliefs.

- **Audio media:** if you listen to the radio, you will already be aware of the power of sound. Gentle background noise can filter through and register quite easily. Even though you may be concentrating on other things, your brain is hard-wired to register sound.

• **Visual media**: leaflets, newspapers, and magazines may seem old fashioned, but they still play a role in PYSOP. They use visual images to appeal to our base instincts and influence our thoughts.

• **Online sources**: of course, the internet and online influences cannot be ignored. As we spend more time looking at screens, the chance to influence our thoughts increases.

Understanding psychological warfare means understanding its role in battle, the quintessential arena for enemies, and conflict.

Typical Tactics of PSYOP

• **Printed leaflets:** using printed leaflets to suggest the enemy should withdraw from the battlefield. Distributing simple leaflets with a strong message that surrender is their only choice will plant seeds of doubt within tired and battle-weary combatants. Instructions on how to surrender safely will often be accompanied by an assurance that no harm will come to them.

• **Overkill:** the enemy can often be convinced of their weaknesses by witnessing a massive attack from the opposing side. Employing a vast number of troops with advanced weaponry will often result in low morale and feelings of defeat for the other side.

• **Sleep deprivation:** this simple yet effective method involves projecting loud annoying sounds or rock music into the enemy's camp. This leads to a lack of sleep, which renders the troops ineffective and lackluster.

• **Enhanced rumors:** if the enemy believes you have advanced weapons that are chemical or biological, it can be just as effective as having them. Creating a perceived threat that has devastating effects will make them rethink their strategies.

• **"False flag" events:** if one side can convince its enemy that it has allies, this can be a turning point in any war or battle. Creating events and attacks that appear to have been carried out by fresh combatants can make the enemy feel overwhelmed and defeated.

Early Examples of Psychological Warfare

Since prehistoric times humans have understood the importance of gaining the upper hand in battle, by deploying some ingenious methods to lower the enemy's morale and weaken their spirits.

- **The Aztec death whistles:** in the late 1990s, archaeologists unearthed two skull-shaped instruments in Mexico. A temple dedicated to the wind god revealed the skeleton of a sacrificed man clutching the two objects. They were identified as "death whistles" often used to intimidate the enemy in battle. Reported to have sounded like the "scream of a thousand corpses," the whistles were used to unnerve the enemy and break their resolve.

- **Sacred shields:** in 525 BC, Emperor Cambyses II of Persia used the Egyptians' love of cats to defeat them at the Battle of Pelusium. The front line of the Persian soldiers included dogs, cats, and sheep as hostages. It is also reported that soldiers drew cats on their shields and pinned real cats to their armor. All these animals were revered by the Egyptians, which made them hesitate to attack.

- **Visual terror of Timur:** in the 14th century, the Muslim world and parts of Asia were ruled by Tamerlane, also known as "Timur the lame", a leader that was crippled by paralysis. It is reported that he beheaded his enemies and used their skills to build pyramids. Tamerlane is credited with some of the most effective terror tactics witnessed by the ancient world. Following his triumph over the Ottoman Empire, he locked the sultan in a cage and displayed him in his living quarters.

- **Vlad the Impaler:** often thought to be the inspiration for Bram Stoker's character "Dracula", Vlad the Impaler understood the importance of psychological warfare as far back as the 15th century. He was often faced with forces that were larger and more powerful than his own, but he knew how to fight with limited resources. Impaling corpses on spikes proved an effective way of striking terror into even the most formidable opponents.

- **Genghis Khan**: one of the most effective exponents of psychological warfare, Khan understood how to use misinformation to fool his enemies. He exaggerated the size of his forces and used horse-mounted dummies to reinforce the effect. He employed kettledrums to shatter his opponent's eardrums and prevent them from sleeping. He had spies in all camps and without fail knew more about his opponents than his enemies did of him. The Mongols became a mythical force that was prepared to kill huge numbers of troops and civilians alike.

Modern Use of Psychological Warfare

The first significant use of PSYOPS in the 20th century occurred during WWI. By the time the war was underway, it was quickly understood that tactics could be used to make the rest of the world more sympathetic to the British. Britain had a strong network that was used to create cross-cultural communications to succeed in the battle for good relations.

Britain also had an extensive diplomatic service that had previously worked with other nations successfully. The Germans, however, had previously tried to incite revolutions in various parts of the world that led to opinion becoming unfavorable.

Early in the war, A Propaganda Agency was formed that included some of the literary greats of the age. Luminaries, including Rudyard Kipling, Thomas Hardy, and other noteworthy authors, composed several publications to convince the world that Britain was the "good guys." The pamphlets listed atrocities committed against ordinary citizens by the German forces and were illustrated with emotionally charged images to support the information. These leaflets were distributed across neutral territories to encourage nations to join them in their struggle.

Later in the conflict, the agency changed tack. It concentrated on targeting the German troops who had spent many long years in atrocious conditions in the trenches. The leaflets were designed to look as if prisoners of war held in Britain had written them. It portrayed a vision of humane conditions, good food, and clean clothes. It urged the soldiers to surrender and told stories of the German hierarchy eating well and living the high life. It is thought that over 25 million of these leaflets were printed and distributed throughout the conflict.

The British were not alone in employing these tactics. French leaders took control of the nation's media and used it to create articles and leaflets that berated the German forces and government. France worked hand in hand with their European counterparts to create bad feelings toward the German forces. It is believed that the Germans discovered the power of PSYOPS a lot later. They succeeded in creating good feelings by giving Lenin, a Russian revolutionary, free travel on a secure train following the defeat of the Tzar. This action led to Russia withdrawing from the war soon after.

PSYOPS Used in WWII

Just a few decades later, the world was once again in conflict. Throughout the war, the Axis and the Allies engaged in prolonged use of propaganda aimed at the psychological manipulation of the enemy. No longer was war a test of superior weaponry and armed troops. It involved the manipulation of the worst and most vulnerable parts of the human psyche to systematically reduce soldiers to their knees until they were too demoralized to fight.

Leaflets depicting marital infidelity and images of families being torn apart by the war were distributed. These were designed to increase the insecurity felt by soldiers who had wives and loved ones back home. Hitler first introduced the use of trained psychologists to aid his war efforts, but Britain was quick to join in the race for psychological dominance.

The science of combat psychiatry emerged, and the psychological effects of warfare on the individual were listed for the first time.

It was discovered that the stresses of war consist of five different stages which are:

1) Pain.

2) Cold.

3) Hunger and thirst.

4) Fatigue.

5) Boredom and loneliness.

Initially, troops are gung-ho about going into battle and filled with nervous enthusiasm. As they enter the combat zone, there is a sense of resignation. They begin to feel a sense of their own mortality and become depressed. They are in a strange place, surrounded by the noise and the smells of the battlefield. As the process continues, they begin to think about family back home. The environment they are facing day in and day out becomes overwhelming, and they sink further into depression. This is when they are vulnerable to psychological warfare, and both combatants realized this early in the conflict.

Radio propaganda emerged from all sides accompanied by printed leaflets, newspapers, and news sheets. The Allies used motion pictures, emotionally charged images, and radio campaigns to infiltrate the enemy home fronts.

As the US entered the conflict, the propaganda level was raised considerably. The Japanese were also adept at PSYOPS, and every campaign in the Pacific theater was enhanced by a form of PSYOPS on both sides.

Possibly the most controversial form of psychological warfare was the bombing of Pearl Harbor in Hawaii by the Japanese. The attack was designed to demoralize the US and make them leave the conflict. The Japanese thought that such a bold move would make the US back off and leave the Allies to fight alone. This was possibly the biggest mistake of the whole conflict. The attack awakened the fighting spirit of the US and led to a sweeping campaign that targeted the Pacific Islands. The bombing of Hiroshima and Nagasaki finally brought the curtain down on the war and saw the Allies emerge triumphantly.

Iraq and the Weapons of Mass Destruction

More recently, the citizens of the US and the UK were subjected to a campaign of misinformation, stating that Iraq held "weapons of mass destruction." This led to the invasion of Iraq, based on "evidence" apparently held by the Governments of both countries. This information came from the highest level of government in both nations, and the call for war seemed inevitable.

This form of PSYOPS is used to manipulate the public into supporting governmental policies that would otherwise be repellant. Did the government genuinely believe that these weapons existed, or did they use the claim to manipulate the public?

PSYOPS in Everyday Life

The actions we take and the words we speak will always affect other people to some extent. But are we subject to a higher level of psychological manipulation? The simple answer is *yes*.

Take advertising. The images you see, and the products you view are all carefully placed to encourage you to buy. Attractive people are used to make you want the life or belongings they are advertising. By using models to market a product, you are led to believe you will appear more attractive when you buy that particular product.

Assertive language is used by advertisers and the media to encourage people to conform. They use phrases designed to make the customer feel better about themselves. Using "assertive language" involves being both persuasive and empathetic at the same time.

A workplace is also a place where psychological methods will be used to manipulate you. This is not always a bad thing. A great manager will be able to use psychological conditioning to encourage team members and get the best from them. Bad managers will use aggressive forms of manipulation that can result in the opposite effect.

The truth is that psychological triggers surround us. This should not make us nervous or paranoid, but we should be aware that manipulation is part of our daily lives. Learn how to spot truthful information and discount the manufactured information presented to you.

Chapter 2: It All Starts with Dark Personalities

Now we delve into the world of human personalities. Our behavior and personalities are what shape us as human beings, and people exhibiting dark personality traits have been described as part of the "Dark Triad." This is a term coined by psychologists for people who are prone to manipulating and deceiving others to get their own way.

The Dark Triad is a term used to describe the three personality traits that indicate a "dark" personality.

Three Personality Traits

1) Narcissism. Some of the less obvious signs of a narcissist are:

- They are likable: classic narcissists will give a great first impression. They are confident and charismatic.

- They will be found in leadership roles: that is not to say that they make good leaders, but they will be happier to take on the role. Narcissists will be more self-possessed and, therefore, more likely to apply for promotions.

- They always manage to turn the conversation toward themselves: it wouldn't matter if you had the most exciting news ever, within minutes, the conversation will be about them.

• They refuse to take the blame: when a narcissist is talking about themselves, it will normally be about their successes and triumphs. Even when the story involves failure, it will never be the narcissist's fault.

• They love to look good: narcissists will make the most of their appearance and will be well-groomed. This doesn't mean that all attractive people or those who take pride in their appearance are narcissists.

• They surround themselves with the best: material items are very important to narcissists, and they love to display them. One example of narcissism is the person who drives up in a Maserati, yet tells you what a great deal they got on the price!

• Media presence: how they appear to others is ultra-important to narcissists. They will be aware of every image on their social media, and it will not contain a single bad picture. They will have a wide range of friends and spend lots of time maintaining their online presence.

• Everything is personal: a narcissist will not welcome any form of criticism. It will be an affront to their self-image, and they will not react well.

• They struggle to keep relationships: narcissists are constantly looking to improve the person they are with and so are more likely to cheat. They will have a history of failed relationships and infidelity.

2) **Machiavellianism**. The common traits of this personality disorder are:

• Self-focus: they are solely focused on their own ambitions and interests.

• They use flattery to win over others: they are so self-assured that even the most blatant lies can be interpreted as flattery. They persuade other people that they admire them and find them special.

• Can come across as difficult to engage: when talking to someone, they will often be distracted by other conversations or events. This is because they believe that everyone else is below them and that there is something more interesting elsewhere.

• They lie effortlessly: their moral compass is totally skewed. They believe that the end justifies the means, and any lie they tell is perfectly acceptable.

• They lack morals and principles: normal social conventions are for mugs. They believe they have a given right to behave within their own personal moral boundaries.

• Lack of empathy: they fail to understand that other people matter or that their actions affect other people emotionally. People with Machiavellian traits will be unable to show sympathy or remorse. They can't connect with people or comfort them when needed.

• Failure to maintain relationships: nobody is good enough for them, so they are constantly seeking to improve their partner.

• Prone to casual sexual encounters without guilt: they don't believe that infidelity is wrong. They simply see an opportunity to have sex with someone as self-satisfying and gratifying. They will cheat on partners regularly, and this is part of the reason they are unable to maintain relationships.

• Can display high levels of patience: their calculating nature means that they see opportunity with every encounter. This means that they can be more willing to show patience with people or situations that may prove valuable to them in the future.

- Prioritize material objects over personal relationships: the big house and the flash car will be much more important to them than a loving partner or happy family. Machiavellian people are all about the impression they give to others and how people perceive them.

Put quite simply, Machiavellian personalities are selfish, self-obsessed, and quite unaware of the needs of others.

3) Psychopathy. The common traits of a psychopath are:

- An enhanced sense of self-importance: even the smallest throwaway compliment will serve to inflate their ego.

- Requires constant stimulation: psychopaths are notoriously hard to engage. They will find quite calming situations difficult to maintain. They are constantly looking for the next moment of danger or excitement.

- Never says sorry: they believe that all their actions are justified, so why would they need to apologize. They are completely unaware of other people's emotions or feelings.

- Lack of remorse: in the mind of the psychopath, once an action is committed, it becomes redundant. They are immediately seeking the next thrill or emotional high. When their actions are questioned, they genuinely can't summon up remorse. They have no concept of contrition.

- Promiscuous sex life: sex provides them with a bolt of adrenaline, so they are constantly looking for sexual encounters. Psychopaths will often try sex with partners from both sexes as it is less about the physical encounter but more about the boost to their ego. They will seek encounters that provide them with danger and excitement.

- Lack of emotion: they have no emotions but can be adept at faking them. They understand the importance that other people place in emotional displays and can be convincing when required.

- Lack of restraint: part of the lack of emotion is an overwhelming absence of fear. If you have no fear, then boundaries are lowered. Why would you not do something if you don't fear it?

- They believe the world owes them a living: they are adept at using charm, flattery, and manipulation to mold people to their will. This will get them a level of success without actually working on a normal level. If they can see a way to improve their own circumstances, they will take it, no matter how it affects others.

- Short term goals and ambitions: they see no point in planning for the future because it is a concept they don't grasp. Psychopaths live in the moment and don't understand long term goals or ambition.

- Prone to overindulgent bursts of temper or rage: if things aren't going their way, it can lead up to a level of stress that they react with violent repercussions. Even the slightest setback can seem devastating as they have no concept of failure and don't know how to deal with it.

- Can be charming when trying to influence others: they understand how to turn on the charm when required.

- Has a history of childhood behavioral problems: they will have been a "problem" child from adolescence? They may have a history of cruelty to other children and animals. Their parents will have found it impossible to control them or discipline them.

- Prone to petty crime: nothing is off bounds for a psychopath. Even the pettiest of crimes will give them a momentary thrill, and they will constantly be seeking that thrill.

In a perfect world, these traits would not be "normal" in successful people, but we all know the world is far from perfect. Narcissists are successful when choosing their mates, even though they lack the skills to form long term relationships. Machiavellian traits are also useful for social manipulation, and when combined with a narcissistic personality, it confers a marked advantage when dating.

The combination of the first two Dark Triad traits is also advantageous for those looking to enter the business world or to become active in politics. People with these traits will be naturally able to manipulate others and pursue their goals with ruthless ambition. They won't worry about who they upset on their journey to success. It is certainly true that those who have inner steel will find their path clears quicker than those with a conscience.

A report printed in the *Journal of Business Ethics* in 2016 stated that the three Dark Triad behaviors work together to allow people to act fraudulently without considering the consequences. In the report titled *The Effects of the Dark Triad on Unethical Behavior*, it was concluded that narcissism motivates individuals to indulge in behaviors that would be unethical to others. The Machiavellianism would then alter the perceptions of the acts and behaviors and give the perpetrator a misplaced sense of justice. Psychopathy would help them rationalize the behavior and remove all feelings of guilt or remorse.

The "D" Factors

Recently published research projects have defined a broader definition of the dark side of human personality. They have coined the phrase "the D factor" to cover some of the other personality traits that are indicative of a dark personality.

The Dark Triad has noticeable differences and can be found individually as well as simultaneously in people, but some other personality traits should be examined.

• **Spitefulness:** anyone who has used the phrase "to cut off one's nose to spite one's face" understands the common conception of spitefulness. It is the willingness to put yourself at the risk of harm to make sure other people suffer.

• **Moral disengagement:** the thought processes employed by a person are different from others and allows the person to behave without any negative emotions. They have no distress, guilt, or shame, even when they behave unethically.

• **Egoism:** not to be confused with egotism, egoism is the ethical theory based on the pursuit of self-interest. Egotism is the overstressing of an individual's worth.

• **Sadism:** the desire to cause pain for pleasure. Sadists believe that they are entitled to cause others pain and suffering, for their own pleasure.

The studies have shown a common factor between all dark personality traits. That is the tendency to place personal goals and interests above anything else. This common core proves a moral justification for distress, pain, and suffering caused to others without any form of emotional repercussions, like remorse. However, all dark personality factors are not the same, and they can result in varying actions and behavior.

How Are Dark Triad Traits Measured?

There are multiple ways to assess if someone has psychological traits that are defined by the Dark Triad. The most popular way is to test an individual with a personal inventory test, to explore the presence of these undesirable traits.

One of the most popular forms of this test was developed in 2010 when two psychologists from Florida collaborated to produce a twelve-question quiz that was nicknamed the "Dirty Dozen."

The questionnaire has four questions per trait. The first four relate to Machiavellianism, the middle four to psychopathy, and the final four to narcissism. The higher the score, the stronger the tendencies.

The first four questions address the individual's attitude to manipulation, flattery, exploitation, and deceit when trying to influence others. The middle four questions involve their attitude to cynicism, morality, remorse, and levels of callousness. The final four questions involve statements about themselves, their self-perception, how others view them, and the importance of prestige and status.

Participants are asked to rate statements with a mark that indicates the relevance they feel the statement holds. The higher the mark, the higher the Dark Triad tendencies. There are multiple tests available online, some are more elaborate, and some are simpler. If you really want to discover just how dark your personality is, then they can give you an indication. Providing you answer honestly, of course!

While the police and law enforcement agencies regularly use these tests to establish the personality traits of suspects, can they prove a helpful aid for other agencies who need to know who they are dealing with?

The military, for instance, has unearthed some interesting data about the presence of the Dark Triad traits in their personnel. The scientific community studied the occurrence of these traits in personnel who carried out war crimes while serving in the military and found a cluster of examples. In both the Iraq and Afghanistan conflicts, there were examples of soldiers carrying out atrocities on civilians while serving in the countries. The systematic abuse of prisoners has been a recurring problem in the military and displays a likelihood that some soldiers have an inner core of darkness.

Of course, it can be argued that anyone who voluntarily signs up for a job that will involve fighting and/or killing other people must have a special set of skills. This is apparent, especially in the military, as the elite soldiers will often present with dark traits. They have the aggression and lack of moral restraint to get the job done—no matter what the consequences. The theatre of war is not the place for regular rules and restrictions, and sometimes personnel with these dark traits are essential for success.

It has been suggested that more stringent testing is required to stop incidents of war crimes and unacceptable behavior. However, there is also research that suggests that military training of cadets is designed to make them more socially dominant and aggressive. Developing a healthy balance is the obvious aim, but improving the standard of military ethics may eliminate some much-needed darker traits that are part of a successful soldier.

So, what can we deduce from the Dark Triad personality types? People with these traits will often initially be successful and reap the rewards from their self-confident approach, coupled with a lack of morals. However, under long term scrutiny, they will be found out. There will be situations of fraud, outright lying, cheating, and general disrepute. It is inevitable we will all have some contact with people who have dark personality traits, and we may even find them charming at first. Recognizing when to cut ties could save you a ton of heartache and give you peace of mind.

Bear in mind that most psychopaths and other Dark Triad personalities make a good first impression. Try and scratch the surface as soon as you can and see what lies under that charming, glossy exterior. You may find a darker underbelly that could become dangerous to you and your sanity.

Chapter 3: The Art of Deception

If somebody tells you that they have never told a lie, then the truth is that they are a liar. While most people are generally honest, the average person lies at least once a day. Deception is a common form of communication, and we all engage in it. Some lies are huge, while others are deployed to make situations better or to spare someone's feelings.

The truth is that it is difficult to avoid lying. We do it to get what we want. We do it to avoid embarrassing situations. We do it to cover up our mistakes etc. etc. and deception can be a difficult habit to break. However, if you are caught in a lie, it can be destructive. Other people will feel cheated and disappointed by your lies. They will distance themselves from you and encourage others to mistrust you. If you tell the truth whenever possible, you can avoid this social void and lead a happier life.

How to Recognize an Effective Liar

Deception, duplicity, fraudulence, chicanery, and deviousness are the bedrock of a Dark Triad personality. They are adept in social situations and can lie shamelessly.

Here are some other ways to spot an adept liar:

• They are natural performers: think about actors and the job they do. Actors "pretend" to be someone else for a living. They are professional liars. If you are in the company of someone who appears to be performing and talking to an audience, then your radar should be beeping.

• They are manipulative: successful liars can steer conversations and situations to suit their agenda. If a subject crops up that makes them uncomfortable, they will have a strategy to change the subject quickly but without any awkwardness.

• Expressive and attractive: it may seem unfair, but attractive people are trusted more than their less attractive peers. Combine attraction with an animated way of speaking, and you have the perfect storm for a believable liar. Of course, not all pretty people are liars, but try and remember to be more aware when confronted with an attractive and animated person.

• Eloquence: stumbling over your words or filling the conversation with verbal pauses like "hmm" or "uh" is less engaging. An effective liar will avoid meaningless phrases like "you know" or "it's like," as eloquence is more convincing.

• Good recall: liars are often caught out by memory loss. Inconsistencies in a story are the biggest clue when trying to spot a lie.

• Keeping information concealed: when confronted by a pointed question, a seasoned liar will be frugal with details. They will skirt the details and say as little as possible. Using phrases like "I truly can't remember" or "I have no clear recollections" are designed to avoid the need for a constructed lie.

• They will constantly be trying to prove their honesty: honest people don't need to convince you they are honest and will state their facts and information without back up. When someone is lying to you, they may feel the need to assure you of their "honest" intentions. Phrases like "I swear that is true" or "to be perfectly honest" should set alarm bells ringing. If they are emphatic about their honesty, the chances are, they are being dishonest or lying.

- Rehearsed answers: when you ask an honest person a question, they will pause and consider their response. The pause may be just a second or so, but it can tell you volumes. Liars have a script and will have rehearsed their answers beforehand. If someone answers you immediately with an answer that is full of detail and smoothly executed, it could be a lie. Most people would expect liars to be hesitant and unprepared for on the spot questions, when actually the opposite can be true. If you ask someone what they did on holiday last year, honest people will have to take a moment to remember. Slick, polished responses are a giveaway sign of dishonesty.

- Listen for pronouns: liars are constantly trying to distance themselves from their lies. They will avoid using the pronouns "I," "me," and "myself" in conversation. They will refer to themselves in the third person instead. In writing, the most common point of view is often the third person, so the use of it by storytellers is well documented. This makes a lot of sense, as liars are essentially telling you a story, so recognizing this type of speech can be a classic way of identifying a lie.

- Tone and structure: listening to someone's voice can be a great way to spot a lie or liar. When people tell a lie, there can be a slight change in the tone of their voice and how they form sentences. Listen for a higher tone of voice or a lowering of tone. If a person's rate of speech alters, it may mean they are less than truthful. Honest people speak with a constant, measured tone as they have nothing to hide. When the brain is working in overdrive to think up different ways of constructing fresh information, it can forget to regulate speech patterns and tone of voice.

The Body Language of a Liar

The signs someone is lying to you can be difficult to spot, especially if they are a practiced liar. There are no tried and tested ways to determine whether someone is lying with 100% certainty, but there are some signs to watch out for. Verbal clues are important, but body language can tell us even more. How a person reacts to a situation will be harder to control and can give us major clues when someone is lying. Body language accounts for 55% of our perception when communicating with other people.

So, what do we need to look for?

Quick Changes in the Position of Their Head

If you see someone jerking their head right before they answer a question, it could be an indication; they are not truthful. Bowing their head or cocking it to one side is a sure sign that something is amiss. Any sudden movement of the head should be recognized as a potential warning sign that the person is lying.

A Change in Breathing

When you lie, you put pressure on your body, and it will tense up. When people lie, they are both tense and nervous, so this will affect their normal heart rate. It will become elevated, and this, in turn, increases the flow of blood. This will cause the shoulders to become tense and rise from their normal position and cause the person's voice to become shallow. In essence, they are experiencing sensations related to being out of breath, which will change their breathing patterns.

Blushing and Sweating

The symptoms above will also result in a rise in temperature, which could result in red cheeks and a heightened complexion. Sweat on the upper lip is a sure sign of anxiety, as are sweaty palms. Any sign of an increase in temperature without external cause could be a sign of lying.

Lack of Movement

It is a common misconception that people who are lying will fidget. Twitching and nervous movement can just indicate a level of anxiety that is normal. In fact, a lack of movement is a far greater sign that something isn't right. The human body is primed with a fight or flight response, and standing still is the first stage of the fight response.

The body is readying itself for confrontation and will be conserving energy for the up and coming fight. When people speak and engage with others, it is normal to move the body with subtle, relaxed, and mostly unconscious movements. A lack of movement, which leads to a form of catatonic and rigid stance, is a sure sign they are readying themselves for an argument.

They May Touch or Cover Their Mouth

This has been proved to be one of the most telling signs that someone is lying to you. Covering the mouth with a hand is an automatic response to untruths or confrontations. When adults raise their hands and place them in front of their lips or mouth, they are indicating a disengagement from communications. They may be unaware they are making the gesture and carry on the conversation, but you should be warned that their words may contain a measure of untruths.

They May Cover Vulnerable Body Parts

The throat, chest, abdomen, and head are all vulnerable parts of the body. The soft skin in these areas is particularly at danger when under attack. The covering of these areas with a hand indicates a level of attack or fear. This may not apply to liars as such, but it does indicate you have touched a nerve with something you have said. When you are in conversation with people, watch for this telling gesture that will indicate you are causing them concern.

Shuffling of the Feet

A quick look at someone's feet can tell you a lot. We have already touched on the fight or flight response that humans are naturally born with. While the rest of the body may be preparing to fight, shuffling feet are another indication of a potential liar. They are uncomfortable with the situation and are eager to get away.

The Inability to Speak

The automatic nervous system is prone to stress when you lie, and it will cause the saliva in your mouth to dry up. This, in turn, causes the mucous membrane to become dry and fail to work correctly. Watching someone trying to speak and failing can mean this process is heightened. Biting the lip and pursing of the mouth are also unconscious attempts to generate saliva by other means.

Eye Contact

We understand people who fail to maintain eye contact can be viewed as shady. They must have something to hide, right? While this is true, there is another side to the coin. Practiced liars will overcompensate by maintaining an unnatural amount of eye contact. They will use a cold hard stare to try and intimidate you and will often be the last to break contact. Honest people having a natural conversation will occasionally break eye contact and then reengage. This is normal behavior, but liars will try and use a steely gaze to control and manipulate you.

This type of contact can lead to the eyes drying out. Watch for rapid blinking, as this indicates an effort to rehydrate the eyes without breaking contact.

They Will Use Aggressive Gestures

If a liar feels like they are being confronted or are about to get called out, they will attempt to turn the tables with aggression. Pointing at things, thrusting the chin out, and sweeping movements of the arms are all an indication you are getting under their skin. Their face may still be maintaining a measured, calm expression, but any sign of aggression is a sure sign they are getting stressed.

What Are the Different Types of Deception?

The most common form of deception is a direct statement that is not true. Then you have the liars who distort facts to make them appear true. Leaving information out is regarded as the sin of omission. Self-serving lies are all about getting what you want, making yourself look better, and covering up any mistakes. Some people use these types of lies to increase their feelings of self-worth and confidence.

Could I Be Lying to Myself?

Most certainly. Lying is not just an outward-facing process. The lies people tell themselves fall into two different categories. If you are inflating your self-esteem with lies, then you run the risk of failing to address the issues you are facing. This can lead to serious feelings of delusion that can spiral out of control.

On the other hand, there is the thought that lying to yourself about your limits can be a positive way of thinking. Think about it, when you imagine yourself achieving accomplishments that deep down you are far from certain are possible, is this a lie, or is it just a positive mental attitude? Lies are not always black and white, and they will never be totally eradicated from the human psyche.

When considering psychological warfare and the manipulation of others, it is important to understand certain forms of deception. Gaslighting is one of these tactics that falls into the category of ultimate dirty fighting. It is a tactic in which a person or entity makes their victim question every aspect of their being. They manipulate their victims over a period of time until they have total control. It is a form of brainwashing that has been used for centuries and is still alive and well in modern times.

The technique has been used by dictators, cult leaders, and abusers, and can be directed at individuals or groups of people.

So, how well do you think your "BS detector" is working? Can you spot a liar within minutes? The truth is that most of us are confronted with so many lies daily; we have lost the ability to detect deception. The information above should have given you the ability to become a real-life lie spotter. So, here's a test to see what your lie quotient is, your "lie-Q" if you like.

These Twenty Questions Will Assess Your Lie-Q:

1) Which response indicates the highest level of dishonesty?

   a) "To be honest ..."

   b) "To be brutally honest ..."

   c) "Honestly ..."

2) How do you recognize a fake smile?

   a) Lack of action in the muscles around the eyes.

   b) Lack of action in the muscles around the mouth.

   c) Lack of action in the muscles around the jaw.

3) When someone is telling a lie, they will blink rapidly:

   a) True.

   b) False.

   c) Probably.

4) The use of strict chronology will be found in:

   a) A true story.

   b) A false story.

   c) Either type of story.

5) When asked a detailed question, will a dishonest person repeat any details?

   a) No.

   b) They will repeat key details.

   c) They will repeat the whole statement.

6) A deceptive person will avoid eye contact:

   a) Sometimes.

   b) True.

   c) False, they will use excessive eye contact instead.

7) Will a deceptive person answer a random question with a pause?

    a) Sometimes.

    b) Never.

    c) Always.

8) When someone is telling you a lie will they:

    a) Remain still.

    b) Move naturally.

    c) Become over-animated with their movements.

9) If you have caught someone out in a lie should you:

    a) Ask directly what made them lie.

    b) Keep quiet and let them talk.

    c) Ask them what they felt when they lied to you.

10) When someone is lying will you get the most clues from:

    a) Their words.

    b) Their nonverbal communication.

    c) A mixture of the two.

11) A practiced liar will use the following to make them seem viable:

    a) Expressive gestures.

    b) Grandiose statements.

    c) All of the above.

12) When someone covers their throat with their hand, it indicates:

    a) Sincerity.

    b) Lies.

    c) Fear.

13) Practiced liars will:

   a) Use personal pronouns.

   b) Will talk in the second person.

   c) Will use third-person pronouns.

14) If you are questioning someone and their eyes dart to the left, are they telling the truth?

   a) They are telling the truth.

   b) Unsure.

   c) They are lying.

15) If someone is giggling when they answer a question, does this mean they are lying?

   a) Always.

   b) Never.

   c) Sometimes.

16) Do liars use sarcasm?

   a) Always.

   b) Never.

   c) Sometimes.

17) When someone is lying their breathing will:

   a) Become faster.

   b) Slow down.

   c) Remain the same.

18) If someone is lying to a group of people will they place themselves:

   a) At the center of attention.

   b) On the outskirts of the group.

   c) In a place where they have limited interaction with the rest of the group.

19) Does a good liar believe the things they say?

    a) No.

    b) Sometimes.

    c) Yes.

20) Do liars do well in social situations?

    a) Sometimes.

    b) Always.

    c) Never.

While this is just a fun test, it should give you an idea of how switched on your "BS" meter is. Add up the points to see how you scored.

Answers

    1. a) = 3 b) = 5 c) = 1

    2. a) = 3 b) = 5 c) = 1

    3. a) = 5 b) = 1 c) = 3

    4. a) = 1 b) = 5 c) = 3

    5. a) = 1 b) = 3 c) = 5

    6. a) = 3 b) = 1 c) = 5

    7. a) = 3 b) = 5 c) = 1

    8. a) = 5 b) = 1 c) = 3

    9. a) = 3 b) = 5 c) = 1

    10. a) = 1 b) = 3 c) = 5

    11. a) = 1 b) = 3 c) = 5

    12. a) = 1 b) = 5 c) = 3

    13. a) = 1 b) = 3 c) = 5

    14. a) = 1 b) = 3 c) = 5

    15. a) = 1 b) = 3 c) = 5

    16. a) = 1 b) = 5 c) = 3

17. a) = 5 b) = 3 c) = 1

18. a) = 5 b) = 1 c) = 3

19. a) = 1 b) = 3 c) = 5

20. a) = 3 b) = 5 c) = 1

The Results Are as Follows

Under 35: oh dear, you are a trusting soul. Maybe you are one of the innocents of the world and you love the fact that you see the best in people. Life, however, will rear up and bite you on the ass. You need to realize there are some bad people out there and they will tell you lies. Maybe you aren't ready to be a cynical hardnosed member of society, but you do need to sharpen those instincts.

Between 35 and 70: this is the average *lie-Q* category. You understand that you are being lied to regularly, but you have the skills to weed out the really dangerous ones. You may get caught out in some situations, but you will survive!

Over 70: well, hello to the human lie detector! Nobody is getting the best of you any time soon. You can spot "BS" from the outset and won't be taken for a ride by anyone. You may want to rein it in a little, though, as you may come across as cold and cynical at times.

Chapter 4: Psychological Warfare in Relationships

In the following chapters, we will be discussing different tactics in psychological warfare in relationships and at work. One of the most devastating tactics used is known as "gaslighting." Before we delve into the different ways that gaslighting affects a relationship, it is important to understand the basic principles of the insidious process and how destructive it can be.

What Are Gaslighting Tactics?

1) The perpetrator tells outrageous lies. Imagine a lie so blatant being delivered with a straight face. They are setting a precedent. If they can conjure up such a huge lie from the onset, then what can you expect in the future? You are now off-balance and are unsure if anything they say is true.

2) The perpetrator uses complete denial no matter what the situation. When someone is gaslighting you, they will deny everything. Even if you catch them out in a lie, or hear them say something hurtful, they will look you in the eye and deny it. The more they do this, the more you doubt yourself.

3) The perpetrator will use emotional warfare to grind you down. Once they have established what is important to you, they will use this information to destroy you. They will denigrate the things that are the foundation of your being. If you are proud of anything in your life, they will attempt to make it worthless.

4) The perpetrator will slowly wear you down. One of the insidious things about gaslighting is it is done gradually. The perpetrator will take their time and chip away at your defenses with snide comments and lies every so often. They know how to introduce seeds of self-doubt and nourish them with derogatory comments.

5) The perpetrator will change tack and try to be positive. When someone has nothing good to say about you, there is a better chance you will recognize what they are trying to do. When they use positive statements to describe you, they make you question your judgment. This is all about making you rethink your every decision and conclude you imagine things.

6) The perpetrator projects their faults onto you. If you are in a relationship where your partner is cheating, they will often throw the same accusation back at you. This is a deflection tactic at its simplest. When you start to defend yourself, you are distracted from the gaslighter's aberrant behavior, and take your eye off the situation.

7) The perpetrator attracts a posse of "yes men," so-to-speak. Gaslighters recognize people who will stick by them no matter what they do. They will then turn to these people to reiterate their negative comments about you. Common comments such as "see, I told you your behavior was wrong, this person thinks so too," will be used to isolate you. The more people who agree with the gaslighter, the stronger they become. They will lower your defenses until you think they are the only person you can trust. This leads you right back to them, and the power is in their hands.

8) The perpetrator questions your sanity. We all have a fear of being seen as crazy or unhinged. A gaslighter will use the term to put

you down personally and with other people. As you begin to question your sanity, you spiral into self-doubt.

Psychological warfare is not restricted to the battlefield or international conflicts. It surrounds us, and the only way to ensure you don't become a victim is to recognize the tactics.

Relationships form a key part of our lives and can be the most fulfilling, wonderful experiences. Even when relationships break up, you can be left with amazing memories and fondness for your former partner. In a perfect world, we would be able to have successful relationships with amicable breakups and move on to the next chapter of our lives.

Of course, we all know this is not a perfect world, and we will be subject to bad relationships, but what can we do about it?

Recognizing what is happening and dealing with it is the first step to understanding how to improve, heal, or simply walk away from troubled relationships.

Are you ready to empower yourself? Let's consider these classic forms of manipulation and how to deal with them:

1) Bullying: this is the least subtle and easiest to recognize form of manipulation. Your partner will use aggressive tactics to get their own way. For instance, they may ask you to drive them to work and pick them up after. While this may be a normal request, it is the tone of voice that needs to be addressed. Are you given a choice, or is the way in which you are asked threatening? If the latter is true, then you should consider how important this relationship is. Do you feel the aggression may escalate from verbal to physical violence? If the answer is "yes" or even "maybe," then get out immediately.

2) Gaslighting: if any of the gaslighting tactics listed above ring true, then leave straight away. If your partner is constantly trying to mess with your mind and questioning your sanity, they are manipulating you in the worst possible way. This is abuse.

3) Playing the victim: do you find yourself apologizing even when you weren't in the wrong? Your partner is playing the victim. They're using emotional triggers to make you feel bad and to make themselves feel justified. If your partner refuses to take responsibility for their own actions, you must nip this behavior in the bud. Apologize for what *you* have done, but refuse to apologize for their bad behavior.

The best way to do this is to dissect the argument and say something like, "I apologize for becoming angry and raising my voice, but you upset me with your actions. You made me feel bad, and you should apologize for that." Hopefully, this will result in a frank discussion and will clear the air.

4) Convenient neediness: are you constantly taking up the reins in your relationship? Does your partner conveniently feel weak or have a headache when you need help with the housework? Do they suffer from anxiety when you want them to accompany you out to any special occasion? Yet when it is time to go to fun events, they seem to find the energy to go out and have a great time. Unless they have underlying health issues, they are manipulating you by making you feel sorry for them.

Do you really want a relationship with someone you pity? If you are staying in a relationship because you worry about what will happen to your partner if you leave, then this is not a healthy situation. Put yourself first and make plans to leave. If you can arrange a support system for your partner when you leave, it will help. Chances are they will be fine, but you will feel better.

5) Nothing is free: if you feel obligated to your partner whenever they do something for you, then they are manipulating you. In a healthy relationship, you should be able to give and receive gifts and favors without feeling there are strings attached. It is normal to do cool things for each other, but there should be no compulsion to reciprocate.

6) Using your love as a tool to get what they want: do you hear the phrase "If you loved me you would ..." often? Does your partner preempt a request with this phrase? Do they use guilt and emotion to control your responses? If you say no to them, will they revert to statements of emotion to prod and shame you into compliance? If you hear "You would if you loved me," when you say "no" to something, then you need to shut it down.

Try a different method of communication. They may feel it is normal to bring your feelings into a conversation, but it isn't healthy to guilt your partner. Tell them to rein it in and word their requests differently. Tell them you will still take their request seriously, even without emotional manipulation.

You could say something like, "Even if I won't take the car to the garage, it doesn't mean I love you any less" or "I can still love you with all my being without doing everything you ask." Ask for a more direct form of communication and tell them to stop staking your relationship on the most mundane requests.

7) **Emotional blackmail:** this type of manipulation is ugly. It plays on your deepest feelings and makes you a hostage. When someone uses threats and dramatic statements to keep you from leaving, it plays on your basest emotions. When your partner tells you they will die if you leave or that they will kill themselves if you leave, they are blackmailing you.

You are being made to feel responsible for someone else's life, and that is not right. In a healthy relationship, you may feel a partial responsibility for your partner's happiness and well-being, and that's fine. However, you should never feel solely responsible for their life.

In these types of situations, the threats are just that. Empty threats designed to tie you to that person for as long as they want you to remain. They are taking any form of choice away from you and keeping you as an emotional hostage. You may be able to deal with this using couples therapy and counseling to find out why they are acting in this way. Or you could just leave. There is no reason to be cruel, and when your partner threatens to harm themselves, you can promise to get them medical help but distance yourself from any further actions. Tell them you can't deal with them when they threaten self-harm and walk away. It may seem harsh, but you need to stop feeling guilty or responsible.

8) Overusing kindness as a weapon: now, before you dismiss this type of manipulation offhand, try thinking about why your partner is kind to you. Are they using gifts and compliments to coerce you into doing something you don't want? We all know that the beginning of a relationship can be magical. You are both in the honeymoon period, and gifts will be a normal part of your courtship. However, if the gifts and compliments are over the top, consider if they are being used as a form of bribery.

Also, consider if any compliments they pay you have ulterior motives. For instance, if your partner is constantly telling you that you are wasted in your current job, and you should apply for a promotion or seek a better-paid position, there could be two reasons for this. The first reason could be they genuinely believe you are capable of much more and support you in your career. However, they could be trying to manipulate you. If you are perfectly happy in your current job yet your partner is pushing you to change, could it be they are trying to manipulate you into a position that pays better. Do they see your potential salary increase as making their life easier?

9) Forced teaming: in a healthy relationship, you will both have your own opinions, and you will also work well as a team. When one partner is manipulative, they will force you into a forced teaming situation. For instance, if your partner is having a disagreement with one of your friends about politics, they will also speak for you as a unit. "We believe that the Democrats are ...." for example. Now, this is fine if you do have the same political beliefs, but if you have a different view, then they have robbed you of your opinion. When a partner uses this form of tactic, it can become routine and means that you lose your voice and individuality.

If you are constantly hearing the word "we" or phrases like "we are some team" or "we nailed that," and it makes you uncomfortable, then do something about it. Speak up and tell them firmly that you have your own opinions and points of view. If the behavior continues, then you need to halt the relationship and reclaim your independence.

10) The silent treatment: sometimes you can get so mad at someone you just can't find the words to say to them, so you say nothing. And that's fine, you are biding your time and waiting for your anger to subside. But if your partner is using this type of punishment regularly, they are manipulating you.

The Key Signs to Look for to Identify an Unhealthy Use of Silence

- When your partner is refusing to speak to you but is happily talking to other people in the same room. This indicates a sadistic side to their character as they are isolating you and making you feel less worthy.

- If your partner refuses to acknowledge you even when someone else refers to you. For instance, you are at a party, and someone asks your partner if you would like a drink. They then refuse to answer and act as if you don't exist. This is both humiliating and designed to make you feel ashamed.

11) Using humor to shame you: we all have our hang-ups, and your partner will know exactly what pushes your buttons. In a healthy relationship, they will be encouraging to you and help you to overcome your insecurities. If you have problems with your weight or appearance, they will tell you when you look great and make sure you feel good about yourself.

Manipulators will take every opportunity to highlight your insecurities and use them to make you feel bad. Generally, they will couch their remarks in humor and make a joke out of your shortcomings. They are attempting to make you feel inadequate and worthless to maintain their dominance of you. If you feel confident or powerful, then you will find it easier to leave them.

12) They refuse to show emotions: when conflict occurs, a healthy partnership will have a discussion, air their grievances, and come to a resolution. Yes, there may be tears, raised voices, or anger. If your partner refuses to show you their emotions, they are trying to keep you in check. It isn't normal to be cool, calm, and collected all the time. Combine this with comments directed at you, suggesting you are the irrational one, and this is a form of gaslighting.

Remember that having emotions is normal. Try and encourage your partner to express themselves more when conflict occurs. If you can't elicit a response, then it could be time to seek therapy. There may be a deep-seated reason for your partner's lack of emotions.

Whatever the form of manipulation you may be experiencing, chances are you will be aware of the abuse on some level. If there is any hint of a warning bell ringing in your head, the least you can do is have a discussion. It doesn't have to be with your partner; you can try sounding out a trusted friend or family member. Somebody else may have a different perspective on what is happening and could help you to confront reality.

The worst thing you can do is to ignore what is happening and hope that it all gets better. Bad situations will only get worse, and you will get hurt.

Chapter 5: Psychological Warfare at Work

Consider how your normal day is split. Most people spend a third of their life in the workplace, especially on weekdays, so we would like to think it is a place where we can feel comfortable. However, because some people are competitive and, in some cases, spiteful, it can be an uncomfortable and stressful place to be.

If there are people who are displaying personality traits associated with the Dark Triad in your workplace, it can be detrimental to your health as well as your work. They will use unethical tactics to succeed and can be responsible for financial fraud and exploitation of the workplace.

Awareness is your key factor combined with vigilance in the workplace. Identifying colleagues with dark personality traits is not a clear indication of fraudulent practice, but it helps to put things in perspective. Some of the most successful leaders and professionals will display some of the traits indicated by the Dark Triad. For instance, focusing on achievements, self-confidence, and professional skepticism are all personality traits that can lead to career success. The key is to keep the negative aspects in check and avoid questionable behavior.

How to Detect Dark Personality Traits

Consider the following statements and how they apply to the people you work with:

Signs of Narcissism

- Boasting about their leadership skills.
- Routinely comparing themselves to established leaders.
- Constantly asking others for favors.
- Always at the center of attention.
- They only do work that has rewards and recompense.
- Brown nosing when in the company of VIP's.

Signs of Machiavellianism

- They are known for being sneaky and using any method to achieve results.
- They will use flattery inappropriately.
- Lack of empathy for co-workers.
- Regularly caught lying about irrelevant things.
- Can't be trusted to keep secrets and will use the information to belittle people.
- Will manipulate other people to achieve self-promotion.

Signs of Psychopathy

- Will take part in inappropriate behavior whenever possible.
- Has no remorse or morality.
- Will take risks without considering how their actions affect others.
- Has a turbulent lifestyle that appears to be spiraling out of control.
- They have a cruel streak.

- Lack of sensitivity.

We may all recognize at least one trait that could be applied to ourselves, and that is not a reason to panic. Some of the most successful people in present times and history will have a number of these traits. However, they will have a balanced personality overall and will know how to prevent them from becoming dominant.

If you are worried about someone you work with or have recognized any red flag behaviors, you have options. We will discuss these later once we have addressed other potential practices that could prove troubling.

Workplace Bullying

Studies have shown that up to 25% of people will witness some form of workplace bullying during their working lives. While we may feel we can identify people with dark personality traits, bullies can have a different set of behaviors. Some people believe workplace bullying is in your face and defined by individual actions. The truth is that it is normally an insidious way of controlling other people's emotions, psychological and physical behaviors.

Skilled bullies and manipulators can read people and exploit their weaknesses. They understand how to get under people's skin and use techniques to bully them into behaving in a way that suits the perpetrator.

Unfortunately, bullying often goes unnoticed in the workplace and can sometimes be accepted as a "normal" way of getting things done. The slow process of chipping away at an individual's emotional and psychological barriers will often be dismissed as it is difficult to spot and even harder to prove.

Luckily, it is emerging as a subject that needs addressing. No longer are people who are being bullied told to "man up" or "grow a pair" when they bring their grievances to light. Companies realize that this type of practice is growing and should be halted whenever possible.

Bullies are primarily looking to place their victims under duress to cause anxiety. This then leads to feelings of inadequacy, and they are more likely to bow to manipulations.

Classic Signs that Bullying is Occurring in the Workplace

Some bullies will use obvious tactics to intimidate other people and will use the following techniques:

• **Coercion**: verbal attacks can be used to make someone do things they don't want to. Using a loud tone or shouting will cause the victim to feel that they have no choice but to comply.

• **Humiliation**: using insults and embarrassing acts to belittle an employee or work colleague publicly.

• **Aggression**: someone getting up in another person's face can be a terrifying tactic to use in the workplace. It can make retaliation more difficult for the person being bullied, as it can be terrifying for the recipient and can cause excessive anxiety and stress.

• **Invasion of personal space**: if a co-worker is overly familiar or intrusive, it can swiftly lead to uncomfortable feelings. The bully will constantly invade your personal space, and they will feel entitled to tamper with your belongings. This type of bullying is designed to make the victim feel that they have no place to retreat to.

• **Offensive remarks**: we have all known some people who don't respect boundaries. This is a fact of life, but this type of behavior in the workplace can be more than offensive. When someone uses profanities, ribald jokes, or brings up unfounded rumors in public, they make the workplace an unsafe environment. People are entitled to enter their place of work without being subjected to bad language or unsuitable behavior.

• **Negative campaigning**: when a bully decides they want someone to leave their workplace, they can use an overt and underhanded campaign to persuade them to leave. This can be as subtle as a well-placed comment to colleagues about their victim not fitting in or being unfit for the position.

Or it can be as insidious as a full-blown email and online campaign to get the rest of the workforce to agree with them. Leaked emails and social media posts can be used to bully the employee into handing in their notice. The worst part of these campaigns can be the effect they have on the social interactions within the company. People are less likely to join a positive thread online than they are to join a negative campaign. Unfortunately, it is human nature to comment on negativity before positivity.

• **Underwork and overwork:** this type of bullying is quite common. It involves overloading someone with work one day and then starving them of tasks another day. This leads to a confusing state of mind when the employee is unsure if they feel overworked or underused. This will affect their work and lead to mistakes because they're unsure of their position.

• **Keeping a record of mistakes:** we all make them, and we all, hopefully, benefit from them. Mistakes are all part of the work process, but if someone is making notes about another person's worth, then they are bullying them. We are all capable of making our own journals or recording our shortcomings, but when you decide to do it for someone else, you are suggesting they can't recognize their own faults. This leads to feelings of self-doubt, and they begin to question their self-worth.

These subtle behaviors may be happening to you or to someone you work with. Maybe you recognize someone who uses these tactics? Whatever the situation, you need to be aware of the actions and the effects they have on others.

• **Deceit:** plain and simple lies. Do you know someone who is constantly being caught in a lie? Or maybe they are constantly being told lies without realizing it?

- **Diversion:** avoiding tricky subjects or situations when confronted with them. Changing the subject in discussions or canceling meetings and avoiding certain personnel.

- **Creating conflict:** is there someone in your workplace who enjoys pitting people against each other? You know the type; they cause a heated discussion and then walk away. This type of behavior is sneaky and destructive. When the conflict is examined later, they will have made sure their name is not connected to it.

- **Criticism:** we all recognize that constructive criticism is helpful, but unwarranted criticism is aimed at lowering morale. Do you know someone who is constantly putting people down without reason? Do they make inappropriate comments about appearance or personal subjects? This is insidious bullying and cannot be tolerated.

- **Taking credit for other people's work:** some bullies will take advantage of colleagues who may not be as experienced as them to steal their ideas. They will appear charming as they talk about projects and ask the other person what they think. Then they will use the ideas to gain favor and claim the credit.

- **Misinformation:** this is a common form of undermining someone. For instance, if an important meeting has been announced, the bully will "mistakenly" tell a colleague the wrong details. They may even hold back information that is meant to be passed on to make other people look incompetent.

- **Isolation and exclusion:** this is a devastating way of making someone feel uncomfortable in the workplace. We all want to feel part of a team, and being physically or socially excluded will make people doubt their self-worth. A common tactic would be to address members of a group individually while leaving out the intended victim.

- **Minimization:** this practice involves making light of someone's feelings. For instance, if the victim of bullying raises a point about something, the bully will belittle it. By persistently discounting someone's thoughts and ideas, the bully is making their victim shrink into the background and become a shadow.

- **Flattery:** some bullies will seduce their victims by complimenting them and using excessive flattery to make them appear trustworthy. They are offering a false sense of camaraderie and putting themselves in a position of power. If you believe that someone genuinely likes and admires you, then you are more likely to bend to their will.

- **Changing the goalposts:** some bullies in power will distribute titles and promotions at will. They replace different aspects of work without cause and change their responsibilities. This leads to a feeling of unknown and uncertainty. The victim then becomes more vulnerable and subject to manipulation.

- **They give backhanded compliments:** this is such a sneaky way of gaining the upper hand over a potential victim. The perpetrator will set their victim a task. If the task isn't completed, then they will berate them and make them feel ashamed. But if the task is completed, they will react in the following way. "Wow, I never thought you could have done that, well done you!" or "Who would have thought you were capable of that at your age? Great job." This makes them seem benevolent when, in fact, they are delivering stinging comments that will make the victim feel seriously confused. The bully has reinforced their position of having the upper hand while seemingly paying a compliment.

- **They refuse to validate other people:** workplaces should be a creative environment where ideas flow freely and receive the attention they deserve. Bullies will offhandedly dismiss other people's ideas with a cutting comment or a patronizing manner. They will create the impression of benevolence but treat people like children who are incapable of adding value to the workplace.

What to Do if You Recognize that Bullying is Happening in Your Workplace

It is important to realize that attitudes are changing in the workplace. Bullying is no longer tolerated, and there are more litigious claims regarding bullying than there has ever been. With this in mind, most organizations realize that good workplace culture is a solution to costly, time-consuming legal battles.

Here Are Some Great Tips to Help You Prevent Bullying in the Workplace

1) Create a clear policy: there should be no gray areas about who is responsible for dealing with bullying. Human resources should have resources that deal with bullying behavior, and the consequences should be clear.

2) Train senior staff to recognize potential situations: the best place to deal with bullying is at a grassroots level. Once a situation has escalated, it may snowball until it becomes more serious. Having intuitive people in minor management will help to set alarm bells ringing earlier.

3) Promote an open-door policy: all employees need to know they have the right to air their views without fear of reprisals.

4) Speak to your employees: having healthy conversations about bullying and the potential harm it can cause is key. If you don't feel qualified, consider employing a professional speaker to address the staff and make them more knowledgeable.

5) Identify unacceptable behaviors: employees need to know that old fashioned subjects like racism, sexism, or any form of discriminatory speech will not be tolerated. Some people feel that if these subjects are used in humor, it is acceptable. Make sure they know that times have changed, and so has the work-based culture.

6) Provide respectful feedback: no issue should go unresolved no matter how petty it may seem. Every employee should have a voice.

7) Document complaints: there should be written documentation of every complaint. This ensures that any recurring behavior is recognized immediately.

Chapter 6: Propaganda I: Political Propaganda

History has given us some amazing examples of propaganda, and two of the most striking forms originate from the Soviet Union and Nazi Germany. The two nations used effective methods of propaganda to influence their citizens into believing that their side of the story was the correct one.

They bombarded the population with varying forms of propaganda designed to persuade them to toe the party line.

Here Are Some of the Ways the Soviet Union Disseminated Propaganda

1) Schools and youth organizations: Stalin and his team of advisors recognized the best way to shape the future was to educate the youth of the present. They formed a program named the Young Pioneers for children aged between ten and fifteen years old, which taught their members to oppose the enemies of socialism. Children in Russia were surrounded by shrines to the Soviet leadership and were encouraged to learn songs and pledges that glorified the Stalin movement. Chilling images of schoolchildren wearing black uniforms while marching with banners were prevalent in the Stalin era.

2) **Media**: poor people in Russia had no way of accessing any form of entertainment, so the Russian propaganda machine used this fact to "educate" them and keep them informed. They installed radios into communal areas for poor people to listen to the news. They used the walls of subway stations to project propaganda films for those who could not afford the entrance fee to theaters.

3) **Propaganda trains**: Stalin soon realized that the use of the railway system was an effective way to reach his people. He authorized the use of propaganda trains filled with printing presses, projection equipment, radios, and public speakers to preach to the masses.

4) **Posters**: the use of posters as propaganda have been a common theme throughout different eras of Russian history. They regularly depicted the "new man," who believed that hard work and severe discipline were the best methods to overcome the more basic instincts of mankind. Images depicted the "common man" as a hero and created a division within the class system.

Common men and women were encouraged to view the bourgeoisie as an enemy. They promoted anti-religion and anti-American feelings, while vilifying the idea of "noble poverty."

5) **The printed word**: Russian people were only allowed to read newspapers that were favorable to the Communist cause. Any stories of crimes against humanity occurring on Russian soil remained unreported. Russian libraries were purged of "deviant" writers, and pre-publication censorship was introduced.

These methods were designed to encourage Russian people to band together and oppose any form of rebellion. People listened and watched the propaganda together and formed like-minded groups. Punishments for non-conformists were swift and harsh. It was impossible to tune out the noise of propaganda, as it was literally everywhere.

Propaganda in Nazi Germany

The emergence of Nazi Germany took political propaganda to a new level. Hitler was a master of propaganda, and he appointed Joseph Goebbels as the head of his campaign to convince the nation that the Nazi Party was seen in a positive light. He was also tasked to ensure the German people had no access to harmful information regarding the Nazi movement.

Goebbels collaborated with Albert Speer, a German architect and urban planner, to work with the SS and the Gestapo to launch a campaign of national "enlightenment." Their first task was to set up the Reich Chamber of Culture in 1933. This body of men dealt with all media sources of information like newspapers, film, and radio. To qualify for a position in the Reich Chamber of Culture, you had to be a member of the Nazi party.

Any disobedience within the organization was brought under control with severe punishments. Censorship was rife, and the Nazis controlled everything that the people read, heard, saw, and experienced. They understood that this was the optimum way to ensure that Hitler became the supreme leader of the German people.

When this happened in January 1933, the Nazi party was already in a position of strength. They felt strong enough to organize the infamous book-burning episodes that occurred just four short months after Hitlers' rise to power. Any book that didn't conform to the Nazi ideal was removed from libraries by loyal Nazi supporters. They were then publicly incinerated in huge piles, cheered on by Nazi followers. These public displays of power fueled the belief that the Nazis controlled the minds of the people.

The production of powerful propaganda films furthered this display of power. The films were made to highlight several issues and bring them to the nation's attention:

- The greatness of Hitler and his vision for the future.

- The Jewish people: the Nazis used beautiful and artistic posters to promote the hatred and fear of Jewish people and other non-conformist groups of people. They used beauty and art to mask the ugliness and hatred of the message they contained.

- The way forward for the future: they promoted the idea of a "master race" that began with "perfect children." Any imperfection was an insult to the Nazi vision of perfection.

- The mistreatment of Germans in Europe: as the approach of WWII became imminent, the Nazis recognized the need to demonize the rest of Europe. They did this by highlighting how badly migrant Germans were being treated in Eastern Europe.

The making of such films was not restricted to serious documentaries or news-based films. While films like *Triumph of the Will* (1935) addressed serious subjects, Goebbels also recognized the power of entertainment propaganda. He commissioned comedies and light entertainment films to give Germany a more human and lighter look.

Goebbels also recognized the power of saturation. He ordered the production of cheap radios so that every German citizen could own a radio. He also ordered loudspeakers to be set up in public, so everyone would hear the word of Hitler.

Before 1933 the Nazi party was the largest in Germany, but it did not have total support. Goebbels changed that fact and made sure Hitler took his place in history with a relentless campaign to win the hearts and minds of the majority of German people. He understood the premise of successful propaganda, and Goebbels is quoted as stating that once someone had succumbed to successful propaganda, they would find it impossible to escape.

Further into their campaign for world dominance, the Nazis recognized the use of other methods of propaganda. They used symbolism to its full extent. The use of the swastika, the salute, and uniforms made sure that people in the street recognized the power they held. While Hitler understood the importance of grandiose titles for his henchmen, he was astute about his own title. He refused to be called President, as he claimed the title was too "august" for him. This appealed to the common person, and Hitler garnered popular approval with this move.

Nazi Germany was a prime example of mass brainwashing. The Nazis used a barrage of information, images, and events to create an environment of hatred and reverence.

Political Propaganda in the US

As one election passes, the preparations for the next one begins. We are constantly being told to give our vote to one candidate or the other for different reasons. While this is a fact that nobody can escape, are we hardwired to believe the propaganda, or are we capable of making an informed vote?

Recognizing the techniques used is the first step to becoming a savvier voter. Let's examine some of the more popular ways that politicians have used propaganda while angling for our vote:

Presidential Ads

We need to travel back to 1952 to witness one of the earliest ad campaigns for a presidential candidate. "Ike for President" was a catch song used to promote Dwight Eisenhower. In 1960 JFK also used a catchy song to head his campaign. These were early examples of a popular method of propaganda called the "Bandwagon" technique.

The Bandwagon Technique

This is a technique that appeals to the masses and makes people feel part of a movement. This type of ad plays on the insecurities of the masses and the desire to belong. Take the example of a different type of ad. If you see a soft drink advert where masses of people are drinking the same product, it immediately makes you want to be part of the community. The presidential songs were catchy and inclusive and appealed to this type of voter.

The Testimonial Technique

Also referred to as the "endorsement" technique. The candidate uses various methods to boost their persona and appeal to a broader audience. These can include endorsements from political hard hitters, media outlets, sportsmen and women, and celebrities. They are believed to be persuasive cues for uninformed voters who have little interest in the candidates' policies or beliefs. They choose to select their preferred candidate by association.

While we are used to seeing politicians sharing the same platforms as famous people, a recent example was back in 2008 when Chuck Norris threw his support behind his preferred candidate. 2008 also witnessed the online-only advertisement by Barack Obama, which featured a host of famous people.

This type of technique can have a negative response. For every positive response, an association with fame can generate, there is the chance of a negative reaction. This is also referred to as a transfer technique. Highlighting the qualities of a well-known person works well with their followers, but they can generate feelings of dislike in the people who aren't so enamored.

Symbolism Technique

This is a method that appeals to a voter's heart. Remember that propaganda is a battle for hearts and minds, and symbolism is all about hearts. When a candidate is trying to appeal to a base feeling of patriotism, they will use all American symbols to stir the emotions. Think soaring eagles, Uncle Sam, good old apple pie, and flags. Lots and lots of flags. There is something about the American stars and stripes that appeals to the voter.

Nobody is suggesting that anyone looks at a picture of a flag next to a candidate and immediately thinks, "Hey, that flag makes me think you will make a great president," but it does talk to the subconscious. Throw in some glittering generalities, and you have an effective form of political propaganda.

Glittering Generalities

These are statements that use vague words and phrases to influence the public. They have no real meaning; they are mostly emotionally appealing and are designed to have a positive effect on the general population. They literally sparkle and make us believe in a better future and a positive outcome.

The words don't just sparkle; they leap out and give a sense of hope. Everything is going to be okay because this candidate says so! These types of statements have been referred to as "name-calling in reverse."

President Obama famously used the words hope, progress, and change to garner the support of America. We are all aware of the significance of the phrase "Make America Great Again" in 2016 and how that glittering generality appealed to certain voters.

The Plain Folk Technique

This is when politicians try to appeal to the man on the street. They may have had Ivy League educations and never known what it is like to "miss out," but politicians know how to appeal to the common person. George Bush and his son George W. Bush knew a thing or two about using the plain folk technique.

They knew that taking a scholastic approach to their speeches would alienate them from most of the population, so they made mistakes. These errors were designed to make them appear spontaneous and in touch with the average person. Telling the public that they are "a man of the people" can be a powerful tool, no matter what the truth.

Stacking the Cards

This type of propaganda may sound harmless, but it can be devastating. The perpetrator will highlight their personal accomplishments and triumphs without addressing any of their failures. They will then proceed to trash their opponent and drag their name through the mud. American politics is a hotbed of card stacking, and the ads used by candidates can be subtle, or they can use distressing images to suggest the opponent is at best useless and at worst evil.

If the images aren't enough, it could be time to use schoolyard tactics. Name-calling is a successful tactic for those not subtle enough to use other methods. Name-calling propaganda is used by governments and the media to describe groups that oppose their beliefs, who will be referred to as "terrorists" or "insurgents," while groups who support the government will be called "freedom fighters" or "activists."

It is little wonder that these tactics will then spill over into the political arena at election time. It has become the default epithet from both the "Left" and "Right" of politics. These tactics have been referred to as "Nazi-style" tactics. Some candidates bully their opponents by launching personal attacks, targeting individuals and giving them labels. We all remember "crooked Hillary," Dick Cheney being referred to as an "attack dog," Barack Obama being incorrectly labeled a "communist," John Kerry a "flip-flopper," and Joe Biden insulted with the nickname "sleepy Joe."

It really doesn't matter if there is any truth behind the accusation or not. The truth is that these sound bites make the new world of media hum. It thrives on the incessant profanity, trash talk, lies, and the general invective created by this type of propaganda.

Chapter 7: Propaganda II: the Manipulative Media

Consider how media-driven the modern world is. We watch news-media oriented programs on the television, the films we watch have hidden messages contained in them, and we are constantly subject to advertising. We communicate via social media, and every search we make online creates relevant advertising.

The term "media manipulation" is not one we use often, but we are all aware of some form of influence. Back in 2002, Sylvain Timsit, a well-respected French author, coined the phrase when he wrote about how political and economic powers use propaganda and other strategies to control the minds of the public. He became one of the first people to explicitly state the influence and control that mass media had on society.

The mass media is the largest form of remote control available. As people relax and prepare to be entertained, the manipulation of their thoughts and behaviors begins. They are presented with nuggets of facts and information that many people readily believe. They then use social media to share their thoughts and give them even more credibility. These "facts" will then be shared using the internet, cell phones, social media sites, and will travel the globe in minutes.

Consider why that information was presented to you in the first instance. Did it have verifiable sources, based on extensive studies and provable scientific facts, for example? Did it appear because the media feels the need to print and promote truths because it is in our best interests? Or do you feel that the information was some form of manipulation?

Some Strategies That the Mass Media Employs

Distraction

In 2014, Russia moved its military forces into the Crimea. There followed a series of events that would lead to alarm in the US and suggest a return to the Cold War era. The referendum held, the following annexation, and imposing of sanctions could cause a panic in the US, which certain agencies were eager to avoid. This story was superseded by the disappearance of Malaysian Airlines flight 370 and the mudslide in Washington State in the US. Classic distraction tactics used to keep the nation successfully focused on other matters. Acts of nature provide the media with certain elements of news. The number of deaths, potential miracles, and grieving relatives filled hours of news coverage.

Gradualism

This is a method that manipulates the public to accept socially unjust actions or events by conditioning them to the news gradually. For instance, if the government was going to close down certain institutions that would lead to layoffs, it would begin a gradual campaign against the institutions. This would consist of negative media stories about mismanagement, losses, drops in sales, and poor stock market figures. This prepares the public to accept the big news without tumult.

Scripting and Omissions

Most people think of *Time* magazine as a hard-hitting, truthful publication that can be trusted to give the people hard facts. It is highly regarded as one of the more relevant publications in the US and has a large readership. While these facts may be a version of the truth, in reality, some may perceive that *Time* magazine sanitizes its covers for US consumption.

It is standard for print magazines to have different covers to appeal to the target audience in different parts of the world.

Time magazine has a US cover, one cover to appeal to Europe and Africa, while the remaining two covers are aimed at Asia and the South Pacific. During the Obama years, *Time* chose to publish a cover depicting Vladimir Putin and his thoughts on the weak state of the US and the strength of the Russian union. Russia and the US have had a rivalry for years, so it is not surprising that he would call the US "weak" and Russia "strong." The heading was about Syria in Washington and defense in Damascus.

In fact, the gist of the headline was the only part of the cover to make the US version. While the other three covers showed the Russian leader, the US cover asked the question, "Is it time to pay college athletes?" and the headline became: "What Putin Wants," and "Syria: Inside the DC War."

Treating the Public like Children

Unbalanced news-reporting that seeks to rile up base instincts of fear, or dumb down serious issues, is a sure sign that some media organizations are determined to keep us under a blanket of ignorance. If biased media owners allowed us to see the cold hard facts, they run the risk of nurturing a generation of free-thinking individuals that are capable of critical thinking. They need us to be submissive, open to manipulation, and incapable of critical decisions that would challenge their power and wealth.

Manufactured Reality-TV

Reality TV shows are highly entertaining and cheap to produce, which is why there are so many on the airwaves. They draw the viewer in with the promise of real-life drama, tears, fights, more tears, and triumphs. They love to take a normal person and make them into a better version of themselves. This appeals to the viewers' psyche and tells them that they too can become a better person.

The truth is that these so-called reality shows are often scripted, or are carefully produced theatrical presentations. They rely on the viewers' gullibility and their ability to suspend belief to gain higher ratings.

Let's look at some of the common tricks that reality shows use to manipulate our beliefs:

• Frankenbiting: this is an industry term for editing clips and creating complete sentences from scratch. The producers will use different clips of conversation to create the content they require.

• The judges have no real power: in shows with a competitive element, there will normally be a clause that robs the judges of all power. As a viewer, we believe the judges are responsible for a particular contestant progressing, but the truth is different. At any point, the producers can step in and block the decision if they feel the decision will harm the show's ratings.

• Lying about schedules and budget: if you have ever watched a DIY show or you love *Extreme Makeover*, then you will know those amazing makeovers can be done in a short time with just a minimum budget. But can they? If a show is telling you that a bathroom renovation can be done in twelve hours for a couple of hundred bucks, chances are that it is a lie. They will have had a professional team working on the project for around ten days before the presenter steps in to film. Oh, and the budget is often completely unrealistic.

• Flawed people make better TV: reality shows know the power of portraying flawed people and exploiting their weaknesses. It allows the audience to feel superior and thankful for their lives and lifestyle. The producers will delve into the past of participants to discover what buttons to push. They will shamelessly use the contestant's personal experiences to trigger reactions. Unfortunately, because these people want to be on TV so badly, they will sign contracts that allow such intrusive behavior.

Digital Image Manipulation

During foreign or domestic conflicts, it is important to get a balanced view of the situation and decide for ourselves the merits of the decisions being made, right? The media have other ideas. They are using our basest emotions to influence our thoughts. Newspapers and news outlets around the world are at times guilty of manipulating images to influence public opinion. The ethics of digital manipulation is a gray area. You should be aware that sometimes the camera does lie.

Propaganda in Advertising

We have already discussed the role of propaganda in politics, so what techniques cross the stream with advertisers? Well, most of them! Think about it; politicians are trying to sell you the dream, the utopia they can supply if only you vote for them. Advertisers are doing the same. Your life will improve if you buy or subscribe to their product, so they use similar tactics as politicians.

Here are some ways they manipulate the public with advertising strategies:

Testimonial Propaganda

Just as politicians attach themselves to celebrities, so do advertisers. If Jennifer Aniston tells you that she uses a shampoo, then you immediately imagine yourself with shiny flowing locks just like her!

Another example was the Nike campaign to sell the world's best ball. Who do they have holding the ball in the advert? Wayne

Rooney, a well-known soccer player who will represent the best and appeal to the customer.

This technique doesn't just involve celebrities. If you see someone in a white coat promoting toothpaste, you will immediately presume that they are a dentist. They have a professional air about them and a white beaming smile, of course you can trust them!

Bandwagon Propaganda

If you have ever been swayed by public opinion or peer pressure, you understand the bandwagon technique. You don't want to be left out, so you go with the majority. Advertisers realize this and take advantage of the fact.

A classic example is the golden arches of McDonald's. The red sign has the name of McDonald's with a statement underneath that reads "over ninety-nine billion served," which suggests a level of excellence. After all, if ninety-nine billion people have tasted their burgers, there must be something remarkable about them. So, who are you to argue?

Name-Calling

Just as the idea of politicians resorting to playground tactics should be ridiculous, so should this tactic in advertising. However, if a company stays within advertising rules, they can use this tactic without seeming harsh or mean.

If you have ever been in a situation where you are in direct competition with another individual, you will recognize the power of comparison. You may find that pointing out how you are better than your rival is a tactic that works. It may feel a bit mean, but it works so you can use it, right?

Similarly, in advertising, it is common to use a rival to highlight the different ways your product is better.

Once again, we turn to McDonald's for an example. However, in this example, they are the rival. Burger King showed an image of their Whopper burger sitting on top of a burger box. The slogan read,

"Silly Whopper, that's a big mac box," conveying the message that the Burger King burger was too big to fit in the big mac box. Clever or sly? You decide!

Let's try another example. Select Harvest created a noodle product that was free from MSG. Now, they could have used that fact to promote their product and help people eat healthier, but they took another route. They pitted their product against a competitor that still had MSG listed as an ingredient. The tag line read, "How do you like your noodles? With or without MSG?" By posing the question, they are telling you that you, the customer, are responsible for deciding to eat healthily or for filling your diet with the harmful additive MSG. Powerful marketing with a moral twist.

Card Stacking

This type of propaganda has been used for generations and is one of the most common tactics in advertising. Highlighting the great qualities of a product while skirting any negative aspects make items more attractive.

How do they do this? Bold statements that shout about the superiority of a product are common. "This type of chip contains 30% less fat than regular chips." While that may be true, it doesn't make it a healthy option. However, the advertisement makes it look like some form of healthy foodstuff!

Cleaning products that claim to be 50% stronger than the original and have long-lasting qualities will fly off the shelves. Let's consider what the message is. Was the original product so bad that even a 50% increase in performance doesn't mean it will be brilliant? Who knows? These glib statements are meant to catch your eye and distract you from other products. If you buy the product, the job is done!

The truth is that propaganda is biased information and should be treated as such. Advertisers and the media are looking to control your thoughts and emotions to create the outcome they require. It's time to take our blinkers off and welcome a higher degree of truth into our lives.

Chapter 8: Mind Control and Brainwashing

When we think of mind control or brainwashing, it can seem like a concept straight from Hollywood. Images of mad professors with a hypnotic spinning spiral trying to make their patients fall under their spell. The attaching of helmets with electrical cables forcing the victim to become a drooling mind-dead zombie.

In reality, mind control techniques are commonplace in society, and we are subject to them every day. When mind control is used, the recipient may not know they are being manipulated as the techniques are subtle and sophisticated. Mind control is often a lengthy process that gradually changes a person's mind and makes them more susceptible to alternative ideas.

There is no physical force involved. Mind control is a relentless psychological process that applies social pressure on the victim to gain control of their thoughts. Everyone is susceptible to mind control, and that is what makes it one of the most dangerous forms of psychological warfare used today.

Brainwashing is a more aggressive process as the victim will be aware that they are being manipulated. They will understand that force is being applied to make them change their thoughts to align with the aggressor.

However, the early use of the word "brainwashing" was literal. In the early part of the 20th century, there were reports that the medical use of the term brainwashing actually meant washing the brain to cure certain illnesses. In 1934 *The Manhattan Mercury* reported a doctor recommending a patient should "begin with brainwashing. Every brain ... needs cleaning at some point."

In 1935 there was a medical exhibition based on the case of a young boy that had formerly suffered from the condition St. Vitus Dance. He was partially paralyzed, incapable of speech, and prone to fits. His brain was washed twice during four days of treatment, and the boy was cured.

With the dawn of the 1950s came a resurgence of the term. The meaning had changed somewhat, but the term resonated with people looking to describe totalitarian regimes. *The New York Times* reported cases of resistance fighters using the technique to transform weaker members of society into believers of their cause.

As the decade progressed, the term grew more popular. It became a popular way to describe consumers and gullible people who were being duped by advertisers to buy stuff they didn't need.

One of the earliest records of this use of the word is in *The Washington Post* in 1955. It describes how American children had been "brainwashed" into revering Davy Crockett, who was apparently a bad role model as he was basically a juvenile delinquent.

The use of the term brainwashing has now become more commonplace and is used to describe gentle persuasion by propaganda as well as the forced indoctrination meaning of the word.

Who Would Be Interested in Brainwashing?

Mental control is widely used to influence our thoughts and suggest certain ways of thinking, but is brainwashing still prevalent today? The simple answer is yes. We have already discussed the psychological warfare tactics we face every day, so realistically we are constantly being subjected to brainwashing techniques.

There is a fine line between mind control and brainwashing in modern society. Anything that attempts to bypass your thought processes and flip a switch that compels you to obey could be classed as brainwashing.

Manipulation Techniques

Chanting

There are parts of your brain dedicated to analytical thinking. One way to stop this process is to distract the mind with a repetitive phrase. The idea is to shut down any nagging thoughts that will make you doubt the message you are being bombarded with. During recent political conventions, the audience is encouraged to fill the gaps between speakers with repetitive chants. This stops the audience from having the chance to analyze exactly what the speaker has just said.

Planting the Seed

When you scan the internet for news or stories, you will be familiar with short, punchy headlines that tell you all you need to know. The people funding these stories have realized that very few people read the stories and are more likely to skim the headlines. They exploit this fact by planting keywords in the headlines that will manipulate your ideas.

For instance, if the opponents of a certain senator wish to denigrate his character, they can plant a headline that has come from an anonymous source.

Senator White: Cheating On His Wife For A Decade?

It is irrelevant that the statement is merely a question. The seed has been planted. Even if the following headlines appear, it will still have the same outcome.

Senator White Denies Affair

The Wife Of Senator White Confirms Rumors Of Affair Are False

If you are asked if you know who Senator White is, you will probably answer, "The guy who had an affair for ten years right?"

Repetition and Ridicule Fallacy

If you hear something enough times, you will believe it. No matter how ridiculous, if you are presented with "facts" in a certain way, you are hardwired to believe them. This is known as the appeal to ridicule fallacy.

Mocking an idea makes it less relevant. If you associate an idea, a person, or behavior with ridicule and shame, you will dismiss it. Alternatively, if a ridiculous idea is given gravitas and treated with reverence, it will seem more viable. Repetition is a powerful tool, and when teamed with a shaming technique, it can be effective.

Limiting Choices to Black and White Options

When we are put under stress, our brains revert to the fight or flight mode. This is a classic example of having only a black or white choice. When confronted with just two options, we will happily abandon our critical thinking circuitry and make a right or wrong move.

How many times have you seen arguments along the lines of?

"Do we fight the terrorists, or do we roll over and die like cowards?"

"Shall we all get loaded and go to a club, or are you a boring killjoy who doesn't know how to have fun?"

"You oppose the death penalty? So, you believe we should just let murderers roam free and kill again then?"

Using these types of "non-arguments" can trigger humans to shut down critical thinking—compelling them to "take the bait" so to speak, like trained dogs. It isn't subtle, but it appeals to the primitive part of the mind.

Mind Control in the Drug Industry

If you watched the movie *The Matrix* (1999), you might remember a scene when Neo had to choose between a blue and a red pill. The red pill represented his return to the real world, while the blue pill would send him back to sleep. Now, this is a classic case of using a simplistic metaphor to deliver a message to a cinematic audience, but it does have relevance in real life.

When you go to the pharmacy, you are subject to a form of mind control that is subtle but extremely effective. Pharmaceutical companies have used color to suggest an effect for decades.

Take the example of sleeping pills or aids to encourage better sleep. Look at the color of the pills and the packaging. Blue, blue, and bluer. Throw in a couple of fluffy white clouds, with a hint of blue, and the patient is already feeling drowsy.

In one study, patients were given the same sedative, but the color of the pill was changed. Half the patients took a blue colored version while the other half took an orange-colored version. The patients with the blue pills reported falling asleep 30 minutes sooner and sleeping an extra 30 minutes. This extension of a placebo effect suggests that if a patient is given the correct color of the drug, then the results will be improved.

Of course, governmental use of mind control is restricted by boundaries, and government agencies have never used sinister methods to control the minds of the nation. Or have they? Back in 1952, the US was undergoing a troubling period following the Korean War. It was widely recognized that relations with the Soviet Union were strained, and the conflict had entered a new field of battle. The war had progressed to include the battle of the mind.

The CIA appointed Allen Dulles as director in 1953. He coined the phrase "brain warfare" and hinted at the need to expand the methods used to deal with the Soviet threat.

In 1953 the MK-Ultra Program was approved. This highly confidential program expanded the boundaries used to extract information from enemy agents and ensure they were unable to retaliate. They would use biological materials on their subjects as well as some chemical solutions. They approved the use of sexual forms of abuse and torture to gain results. Mind control methods such as isolation, extreme hypnosis, and deprivation methods were all considered suitable and effective.

The prime objective of the program was to develop a truth serum that would work effectively alongside other tried and trusted methods of extracting information. Proponents of the program attempted to use hypnosis combined with the effects of hallucinatory drugs like LSD to help their subjects recall even the most complicated details of physical objects or complicated information.

The use of LSD was perfect for the results they needed. Its chemical effects produced mental states that broke down the subject's character and left them unable to handle stress and anxiety. This allowed the operative to probe deeper without any resistance and gain the information they needed.

It has been reported that following the approval of the MK-Ultra program that over 150 human experiments were carried out using psychedelic drugs, paralytics, and electroshock therapy.

The objectives of the illicit program were clear. They intended to create substances that would:

- Heighten the subject's mental activity.

- Break down any barriers that would prevent them from disclosing information.

- Create a temporary or permanent state of amnesia.

- Enhance feelings of shock and confusion during interrogations.

- Produce temporary paralysis for shock value.

- Use isolation techniques to cause the recipient to become dependent on their captor.

- Lower self-esteem and create a feeling of worthlessness.

- Distort the subject's senses.

- Render them incapable of physical activity.

The other benefit of the program was to make American agents less susceptible to similar tactics if the enemy captured them.

As the program progressed, studies at some of the top universities in America conducted tests on LSD and deemed it too unpredictable for use in the program. MK-Ultra then sanctioned the use of ecstasy or MDMA, heroin, and other class A drugs.

Operation Midnight Climax

The project started in 1954 and involved a web of safe houses scattered around the country run by the CIA. It used prostitutes to lure clients back to the houses and dose them with a series of psychedelic drugs, including LSD. It is reported that the CIA allocated a whopping 6% of its overall budget to fund the program.

The program was conceived to use ordinary citizens to study the effects of these drugs, as recruitment of volunteers was drying up. This highly illegal program involved the prostitutes plying their clients with alcohol spiked with drugs and then having sex with them. Following the sex, CIA personnel would then observe the behavior of the men and use a two-way mirror to tape them for further studying in the future. Tapes of the men having sex with prostitutes ensured their silence. The shame of being found out prevented them from complaining about their treatment at the hands of agents.

Sometimes the sessions took a sinister turn. The experiments conducted on the subjects would often involve torture methods. Doctor Sidney Gottlieb was heading the program, and it is reported he took great pleasure in using sensory deprivation chambers and recording the results. He would then torture the subject further by replaying the most disturbing parts of the recording on a loop.

Some subjects were there consensually, and they were singled out for even more horrific fates than the unsuspecting subjects. Some volunteers were given mind-altering drugs for ten weeks or more without a break.

The MK-Ultra program carried on operating until well into the 1970s under different guises. In 1972 the tide was turning. It was rumored the lid was about to be blown off and the program exposed. The serving director of the CIA at the time ordered that all documentation attached to the program be destroyed.

In 1974 *The New York Times* wrote a damning exposé about the use of drugs and mind control techniques, which led to the formation of a commission to stop this type of experimentation.

The public was formally informed of the existence of such programs by the "Rockefeller Commission," carried out by then US Vice President Nelson Rockefeller. The commission highlighted the use of human subjects to create psychological weapons to use against enemies of the US. It was revealed that at least one fatality had occurred following illegal activities carried out by the program.

In modern times it can seem inconceivable that such methods were used on human subjects. However, times were different then, and it was thought the perceived threat warranted such programs. Now we have much subtler methods of mind control, but who knows what happens behind closed doors? Especially closed laboratory doors!

Chapter 9: How Cults Work

The idea of the cult in the form we recognize is fairly modern. However, the use of the term has been recorded in England as early as the 17th century. The origin of the word is derived from the Latin term "cultus," which means culture or to cultivate. Modern Europe experienced a series of religious upheavals that saw the rise of a slew of new religions. Martin Luther split from the Catholic church and founded Lutheranism, a form of religion that spawned from the beliefs of the Catholic church.

The rise of Protestants in the 17th century led to major upheavals like the Spanish Inquisition. The term "cult" was used to describe the rebels who opposed the more traditional beliefs of Catholicism. The effects were not just religious; it spilled over into artistic and literary circles.

Use of the term then dried up for two centuries until the 19th century, when educated aristocrats and scholars began to take an interest in archaeology and long-lost religious practices.

Novelists soon recognized the appeal of such groups, and the word "cult" entered popular fiction. Any positive connotations soon disappeared, and the term became a byword for religious groups who were controlled by evil and practiced satanic rituals involving sacrifices and demonic worship.

Fast forward to the mid-20th century, and the term cult has become a derogatory way to describe any form of alternative religion or community that doesn't conform to regular beliefs. The alternative "hippie" lifestyle was ripe for embracing "cult" status. The use of drugs and the promotion of free love created a generation of young people who were ripe for exploitation.

Before we explore some of the more infamous cults, it is important to understand them. How they work, why they appeal to some people more than others, and some popular misconceptions.

The most common factor employed by cult leaders is mind control. Most experts agree with this fact and recognize that cults are led by people who are skilled at coercion and employ deceptive recruitment techniques.

Cults take different forms and are designed to appeal to all types of people. After all, a cult is only successful based on its membership.

1) Religious: possibly, the first type of cult experienced back in the 17th century. Religious cults use their belief systems to appeal to potential members and promise spiritual salvation.

2) Commercial based cults: these types of organizations appeal to the base emotion greed. They promise financial rewards if followers do what they are told. They will have a financially successful leader who epitomizes the wealthy future followers can expect. These cults use mind control techniques to persuade followers to work for free. They will produce motivational materials that followers will then pay for. The motivational videos, literature, and seminars will promise them success in the future but fail to mention that the cult leader makes his fortune from selling the motivational materials.

3) Self-help groups: we are constantly told that self-help groups, therapy, and improving our mental health are important. While this is true, some cults will use this fact to target vulnerable people. They may offer expensive courses to "improve your life," which involve being locked away at retreats and subjected to various group activities. They will use manipulative methods to create powerful emotional ties with the subject and validate the power of the cult. This leads to further courses and seminars that promise to advance the individual's improvement and, of course, cost even more. The only escape for many people from these types of cults is bankruptcy.

4) Political: the use of mind control and propaganda by Hitler and Stalin has already been covered earlier. These are classic examples of a cult mentality on a larger scale. Many of these methods have been seen again in recent times, from a number of current political leaders, in the way they seek to control elections and appeal to their "base" of followers.

Common Misconceptions About Cults

When we think about the term cult, it can conjure up certain images. For example, mass suicides of cult members.

These may have some basis in truth, but cults have infiltrated society by taking less obvious forms. If you want to understand the culture of cults, it is essential to recognize common misconceptions as well as truths.

All Cult Members Live in Communes

Cults thrive by using seclusion and isolation to control their members. In some cases, this means physically separating them from the outside world and forming self-sufficient communities. However, some cults are successful at creating a mental form of isolation. They encourage the "them versus us" mentality, which allows members to live and work in everyday neighborhoods and work in regular jobs. These people are emotionally and mentally isolated but present a functioning exterior to mask their fear or hate of outsiders.

All Cult Members Wear Robes, Chant, and Dress in Weird Clothes

Egotistical cult leaders may have guidelines for their members that dictate how they dress. More savvy sects and cults recognize the benefits of blending in. They encourage their congregants to hold down ordinary jobs and use their "normal appearance" to encourage others to show interest in their group.

Cults Are Led By Individuals

The ethos of cults is all about control. While their leaders define the most famous cults, it should not be an exclusive way of defining the term. Often a group led by a board of directors or a circle of "prophets" will use mind control to influence its members. Never dismiss an organization's motives based on its leadership methods.

Cults Encourage Large Families

The popular image of a cult is young girls, pregnant and barefoot with multiple partners and a horde of children surrounding them. Sometimes this will be true; the older generation will recognize the benefits of "homegrown" congregants who are less likely to leave the cult. They may allow multiple marriages and encourage free love.

Some cults operate with a different agenda. They limit or even ban their members from having children. They are more focused on encouraging their members to spend time recruiting new members or working for the group. The control that cults have over their members is what marks a cult, not the type of relationships or size of families.

Cults Are Small and Intimate

In the past, leaders of cults understood the power of personal interaction and influence. Most cults were limited to a certain number of people, hundreds of people normally but never more than a few thousand. Modern communication methods have changed all that. The internet allows cults to appeal to people worldwide, bridging cultural and language barriers with the use of translation apps and social media groups.

Some modern-day cults have used the internet to increase their membership proactively. Groups regularly appear on social media sites like Facebook and Instagram with enticing posts about their teachings and doctrines. The internet is every cult leader's dream; it allows that up close and personal contact they need with people who are thousands of miles away. Some cults have memberships that total hundreds of thousands or even millions, thanks to the internet.

Only Stupid People Join Cults

Having a doctrine that appeals to charitable people draws them in and gives them a sense of belonging. This is when the mind control and exploitation tactics are employed.

Intelligent and successful people often feel isolated because they are different. Joining a cult offers them a place to fit in, to be part of a bigger organization, and to do good. Another appealing aspect of cult life is the power to rise in the ranks. Many cults appoint people to a position of power that allows them to dominate other members, maybe financially or sexually. This appeals to their ego and overinflated sense of self-worth.

Should We Be Afraid of Cults?

When the term cult is used, it can be misleading. There is no meaningful distinction between most religions and cults. They encourage their members to commit to the ideals and beliefs of the group and preach the word to other people. Most religions ask for some form of financial commitment from their members, so why are cults different?

Psychological methods of distorting how their members act, think, and behave are the difference. Studying some of the more infamous cults will help us understand the distinction.

Extreme and Disturbing Cult Movements in Recent History

Sometimes it can seem like the US is the natural home of the cult movement with Charles Manson, L. Ron Hubbard, and David Koresh featuring heavily in historical accounts.

Here we explore some of the best-known cults alongside some of the lesser-known movements from around the world:

Aum Shinrikyo

In 1995 the world was horrified as the Tokyo subway was subjected to a Sarin gas attack. The perpetrators were found to be a Japanese religious group known as Aum Shinrikyo led by its charismatic leader Shoko Asahara. At the time of the attacks, cult membership was estimated to be around 10,000 in Japan and up to 45,000 worldwide.

The movement began as a yoga and meditation class in 1984 and appealed to quiet people who were looking for a spiritual way to practice yogic activities. As Asahara began to grow in popularity, he rebranded the movement and turned the group into a religious cult. He used bold statements, public interviews, and controversial ideas to recruit members. The group began to attract controversy in the following years, and it is reported that a cult member who tried to leave in 1989 was killed.

The group relocated to Western Australia and began to manufacture nerve agents and chemical weapons. It carried out attacks in various Japanese cities, which resulted in many fatalities. Police investigations failed to recognize the involvement of the cult and focused on innocent civilians. Following further atrocities, the involvement of Aum Shinrikyo was discovered, and twelve members of the cult were sentenced to death. Asahara and six other members were executed on the 6th of July 2018, with the remaining members executed twenty days later.

The Unification Church

In the 1940's the Unification Church, or as it is more commonly known, "Mooneyism," began life as a religious movement started by Sun Myung Moon. The group drew beliefs from various sources and recorded them in their "bible" Divine Principle. These were a mix of Christian beliefs, Asian traditions, and focused on the existence of a universal God. They preached the belief that all people deserved salvation, that Jesus was killed by mistake, and the second coming would be hailed by the birth of a male in Korea in the 20th century.

The movement moved its headquarters to the US in the 1950s. It continued to expand until it had reached 5,000 members in the late 1970s. Sun Myung Moon began to proclaim himself as the second coming during this period, and his movement received widespread criticism.

Arguments raged as the parents of young people used deprogrammers to remove their children from the cult. There was also a measure of support in theological circles for the Church, and experts urged a more measured consideration of the practices it carried out. As the Unification Church gained more acceptance in mainstream American culture, Moon was the subject of financial scrutiny by the government.

In 1982 he was convicted of falsifying tax returns and conspiring to defraud the US government. It has been reported that these charges were brought because Moon and his wife had pulled off a huge stunt in July of the same year. They "married" 2075 couples in a "mass wedding ceremony" in Madison Square Gardens while some American members replicated the ceremony in South Korea. Many of the couples were multi-racial and hand-picked by Moon.

In 1994 to mark the 40th anniversary of the founding of the Unification Church, it was announced a new organization would emerge. The Family Federation for World Peace and Unification became a significant force in the religious community and encouraged sexual morality and interracial reconciliation.

The term "Moonies" has become a derogatory term for anyone expressing a desire to join a cult-like movement.

Jonestown

Jim Jones founded the cult movement known as the Peoples Temple. He is infamous because, in 1978, he engineered the biggest mass murder-suicide in American history. Jonestown was a utopian community in the depths of the jungle in South America. On the 18th of November, Jones had led a murderous attack on a U.S congressman and three members of the media in Guyana's capital city Georgetown. Later in the day, he laced a batch of fruit punch with cyanide and urged the members of the group to drink it.

The majority of people complied, although some cult members were thought to have been injected or shot. The expression "drinking the Kool-Aid" relates to what is known as the Jonestown massacre, and it epitomizes the bandwagon form of propaganda and psychological warfare. Over 900 Americans died that fateful day, proving the power of persuasion and mind control can prove deadly.

The Manson Family

Arguably the most famous cult in history was led by Charles Manson, who established a home for his "family" in the San Fernando desert of California in the late 1960s. He encouraged the use of hallucinogenic drugs and the summer of love ethos. Manson proclaimed himself a messiah and encouraged his followers to worship him and follow his every whim. In November 1968, Manson met a showbiz manager who mentioned he was renting his house to showbiz royalty Roman Polanski and his wife, Sharon Tate. Manson formed a plan to send his most trusted devotees on a murderous mission to kill the pair. He planned to spark a race war that would lead to a global apocalypse, allowing him to rise to power.

The Manson Family devotees murdered several victims in 1969, but the most shocking occurred on August 9th. Manson told his followers to murder the pregnant actress Sharon Tate and kill anyone else who was at the property. The four other people at home were murdered alongside the eight-month pregnant actress in a bloodbath that shocked the police officers that attended the crime scene.

The following evening Manson accompanied other members of his family to carry out a further double murder. They tied up and tortured Leno and Rosemary LaBianca at their home in the Los Feliz area of Los Angeles.

The two-day murder spree has become one of the most infamous examples of how dangerous cults really are. So, should we be afraid of cults? We should be informed, aware of the power of cults and sometimes fearful. It doesn't pay to ignore the real and pertinent danger that cults represent.

Chapter 10: NLP and Dark Negotiation Techniques

What is NLP?

The term NLP represents Neuro-Linguistic Programming. In the 1970s, Richard Bandler and John Grinder developed NLP, after studying successful people in the field of communication and negotiation. They discovered the common methods used to persuade and manipulate other people to bend to their will.

This resulted in a program of techniques that concentrate on how the body, the mind, and language work together to provoke certain changes in a person's behavior and make them better negotiators. They discovered how different people grasp the power of language, while others are conscious of more physical behaviors.

NLP works because most people base their reactions on the information available. NLP, as a positive force, assumes that everyone can use the program to achieve their own physical and spiritual goals. It has also been discovered that these same techniques can be used for darker purposes to manipulate other people into doing things they are less than willing to do.

The truth is that NLP can be used with good or bad intentions. If someone is uncertain about progressing with their ambitions or desires, NLP techniques can be used to nudge them forward. If you feel that someone's decision-making process is taking a turn that could be harmful, then the same techniques could alter their decisions. These are good intentions, right? But they can also be used to make people do things that aren't as honorable.

Are You Being Subjected to NLP Techniques?

If you feel that certain people have an unhealthy influence on you and fear they may be manipulating you, it can be uncomfortable. Do you find it impossible to say no to certain people? Are you being manipulated?

Signs That NLP is Being Used

1) They may mirror your actions: pay attention to the people around you. Are they mimicking your body language? When you cross your legs, are they doing the same? Try brushing a strand of hair away from your face and seeing if they do the same movement immediately after. Mirroring is a natural and often instinctive behavior between people who are comfortable with each other, but some people consciously use this as a powerful NLP technique to encourage trust. Some people are more adept at this than others, but if you pay attention, you should notice if the actions seem contrived and insincere.

2) They may use twenty words when one would do: do you have people in your life who use vague, wishy-washy language to say a lot without actually saying anything? For instance, a sentence like "I see you are aware of your personal space and the relevance it has on your physical being, but you are unaware of the barriers you erect to fulfill your self-discipline, while allowing others to float above these barriers and observe you." NLPers love this sort of language, which makes them seem knowledgeable and spiritual at the same time.

3) They insist on rapid decision making: do you have work colleagues who are constantly asking you to make snap decisions? Maybe a boss who pressures you to say yes or no at a moment's notice. Most people need to think things over and take their time making decisions. People using NLP recognize it is easier to manipulate people when you put them under pressure. They will use layered language to influence you like, "We need to make brave decisions quickly; if we don't, we will look incompetent and unprofessional." This type of language is designed to make you feel a lesser person if you don't comply with the initial pressure.

4) They will give you permission to do what _they_ want: this can be a tricky technique to spot. If someone is using it to produce negative results, they will use permission pressure to influence you. For instance, if they want you to give them something, they will pressure you with language: "Go ahead and begin your new selfless life, start with me! Feel free to let go of your selfish nature and share your fortunes with me!"

The idea of these techniques is to make you feel like you are in charge of your own decisions and the paths you choose. They sound twisty and deceitful when you analyze them. Be wary of these techniques and resist being taken advantage of.

Dark Negotiation Techniques

We all must negotiate. It could be as simple as getting your kids to go to bed or as complex as negotiating a new contract at work. Negotiations will play a major part in all our lives. If you know someone who always seems to come out on top when negotiating, the chances are that they know the following tactics and use them to gain the upper hand.

Become Better at Negotiating

Try these negotiation hacks to help you get what you want:

1) Always look disappointed: successful negotiators are aware of the power of disappointment. Even when they are secretly overjoyed with an offer, they know that feigning disappointment will benefit them in the following ways:

- They will be able to ask for more because they seem unhappy with the current proposed deal.

- If they show happiness at the current offer, you may feel you have overstated the deal's worth. This may lead to you reducing or reconsidering the offer.

2) Answer with questions: whenever possible, keep the interaction flowing by using questions to answer queries. For instance, your negotiator may state, "You need to do better than that." You then reply with, "Just how much better?"

3) Point out that defensiveness is not a great quality: if a situation is getting heated, you need to release tension with a laugh. Powerful negotiators recognize the power of humor and will use it to put their opponents on the back foot.

4) Invent a higher authority that dictates what you can do: if you have ever negotiated a price for a car, you will most likely have encountered this technique. Real power negotiators will paint themselves as a low-level operative when it comes to the final say. This means they can halt discussions because they need to consult with a higher authority. You are then left to mull over your offer and reconsider your position. When they return, they can then adopt the good cop, bad cop stance and tell you they did everything they could, but the guys upstairs won't budge.

How to Deal with These Tactics

- Pretend to believe them but make a mental note of the tactic.

- Call the person out on the good cop, bad cop thing.

- Feign interest in meeting the "guys upstairs."

1) Last-minute changes in a deal: creating a last-minute dilemma is a classic manipulation tactic. When a deal isn't struck yet, the other person can claim that a higher authority (possibly referred to as "the board") is interfering with it.

Try this type of blindside in response: "Okay, I hear what you're saying. The trouble is I really want to keep to my side of the deal, but as you were dealing with the board, I had time to crunch some numbers, and the truth is the market has changed. There is more demand for my product, and as such, I will need to charge you a 10% surcharge. I realize this is short notice, so I am willing to drop this to 5%, but I need to know by the end of business today."

2) Use the power of location: you may not realize, but when you are negotiating, whoever is on the home ground has a distinct advantage. If you begin your negotiations by agreeing to meet at their office or their chosen location, you have given the first concession. Try and avoid this by having a say in the meeting venue. A neutral spot will give you an equal playing field.

3) Bringing backup: If you ever feel outnumbered in negotiations, it can mean the opposition is playing negotiation games. If they circle you or all sit opposite you, they are trying to create an antagonistic frame of "us versus you," which is designed to intimidate you.

Try this Powerful Move to Put You in Charge

If more than one person shows up to discuss the deal, try saying this: "Hey [insert name], it is so nice to see you. I was expecting a more personal approach today. The more people that get involved, the more likely it is to get complicated. I can recommend a great coffee shop where these guys can grab a quick drink. It won't take long for us to get this sorted."

Not only have you dismissed the extra people who have shown up, you have taken the upper hand in negotiations and have also suggested that it will be a rapid meeting, and you already know the outcome.

1) The nibbling technique: also known as squeezing the last drop. The more manipulative a negotiator is, the more they will try to get from a deal. Just as you are reaching for the pen to sign the deal, they will drop a bombshell asking for just a little bit extra.

2) Pretend to notice a defect: this is another last-minute tactic designed to elicit extra concessions from you before you sign. They will point out something they claim to have failed to notice and ask for a discount. Stay strong and tell them the price is fixed or try this other negotiation-busting technique. Tell them if they drop the delay tactics, then lunch is on you. Then feel free to walk away immediately after the deal has been sealed.

10) Use online resources to level the playing field: if you are in a position of power when closing a deal, your opponent may stick to electronic mediums to negotiate the outcome. Don't panic, they are trying to get one over on you, but you are aware of their game. Suggest that a face to face meeting should occur, but you can discuss the details online. This helps you gauge their reasons for avoiding personal meetings.

Other NLP Methods

NLP is not just about manipulating other people. It is intended to be a manual for your brain that can transform your life completely.

Try these NLP techniques to manifest a better future for yourself:

1) **Dissociation:** what are the worst-case scenarios you face regularly? Do you panic when faced with public speaking, or get shy

in the presence of members of the opposite sex? Try the following steps to help alleviate these crippling emotions:

- Identify when you are feeling uncomfortable and not fully in charge of your emotions.

- Imagine yourself rising above your physical body and looking down on the situation. You are simply an observer, and your feelings will change as you continue to watch.

- Float back to your physical self and bring the feeling of calm you are experiencing with you. If you feel panic occurring, repeat the process until you feel comfortable.

2) Content reframing: this technique is all about getting things in perspective. For instance, maybe you have lost your job. You may be distressed at first, but you need to change your experience. You are now free to try a different career. You could decide to start your own business, instead of becoming fearful and panicking, focus instead on the positives.

3) Create rapport: you can try to create empathy and connection with another person by mirroring their body language during a discussion. Mirroring will often occur subconsciously between two people who share similar interests or a close bond. Of course, mirroring is just part of the package and won't make people like you if you are a horrible person. It is just a gentle nudge to pay attention and get others to share a rapport with you. If they smile, you smile. If they tilt their head when talking, then you might do the same. Try verbal mirroring and lower your voice when they do. If you pick up certain terms they love to use, then incorporate them into your conversation.

In short, NLP techniques can be used to make yourself a better person. This will help you gain friends and become more confident. You will project an improved version of yourself that others will naturally gravitate towards.

It cannot be stressed enough; the NLP methods can be both positive and negative. How you use these techniques is a personal choice. Be aware that using psychological warfare is a significant way to change people's lives. Use them carefully.

Chapter 11: Cybercriminals

It is important to define the term cybercrime to understand how cybercriminals operate. In 1981 Ian Murphy, who was also known as Captain Zap, became the first person ever to be convicted of computer-related crime. He hacked into AT&T's computers and changed their internal clocks. This allowed customers access to late-night discounts during daylight hours.

Three years later, in 1984, the Secret Service received jurisdiction over computer-based fraud, which led to Congress passing an act that stated hacking into computer systems was considered a criminal act. The first large scale attack was in 1988, when $70 million was stolen from the First Bank of Chicago. This led to a slew of attacks as hackers became more prevalent and successful. Stories of teenage hackers infiltrating government websites appeared in the media, and "hacktivist" groups began to form.

In 2008 the Pentagon officially declared cyberspace the "fifth domain of warfare," which identified the growing threat posed by cybercriminals.

What is Cybercrime?

It is the use of cyber networks to gain illegal access to data and information held by other people. This can include national websites, Governments, corporations, retail online organizations, banks, and individuals. When we use our personal computers, we should be able to feel safe. We should be able to trust that our information is not at risk from fraudulent sources and cybercriminals. This, of course, is seldom the case.

Cybercriminals target anything and everyone. They are interested in anything that can be used to create profit. This could involve trading military or trade secrets, or as simple as the theft of credit card details or PINs for debit cards.

New technologies inevitably create new criminal opportunities, but that doesn't necessarily create new forms of crime. Cybercrime is an online form of theft for traditional criminals who can use a computer. Fraud, child pornography, and identity theft all existed before the emergence of the computer, yet they have all been linked with the umbrella term of cyber-crime.

The important distinction to understand is that cybercrime has a nonlocal character. It has opened worldwide opportunities for those who seek to benefit from criminal activities. The planet-spanning benefit of the internet offers such a vast array of opportunities for criminals; it has created some gray areas of legality. For instance, if a person who lives in a country with strict laws against certain types of pornography then accesses such material in a country that has less stringent laws, are they subject to that country's laws or the ones of their resident country?

Where does cybercrime take place? There are methods for cybercriminals to hide their tracks and disguise their online presence. However, just as traditional police forces can track physical criminals, some cyber professionals are trained to uncover a cybercriminal's tracks.

Common Forms of Cybercrime

Quite simply asking what types of crime are carried out online is like asking a law student to list every type of crime committed in the world. While we are aware of cybercriminals hacking into major organizations and causing worldwide disruption, this often does not affect our daily lives. The crimes most pertinent to individuals often involve some sort of fraud or theft.

Cybercrimes That May Affect You

The Nigerian or the 419 Scams

Before the advent of online crime, this scam was used with both traditional snail mail and later with faxes. The scam involves a request from a "Nigerian prince" who has millions of dollars tied up in an account in Nigeria and needs a bank account to transfer it to. The recipient will be asked for a small upfront fee to help move the money out of the country with the promise of receiving a larger sum in the future. Of course, the money never materializes, and the scammer will often ask for further money, and some victims have been scammed out of hundreds of thousands of dollars.

ATM Fraud

Cybercriminals love a mundane yet simple way to make cash. They have developed a way to record data from customers' cards at the ATM and then they hack the bank records to gain access to PINs. They then create imitation cards to withdraw large amounts of cash illegally. The problem is on the increase, as ATMs are the preferred method of withdrawing cash across the globe. ATM theft has become a growing international problem.

Wire Fraud

We quite happily transfer funds online to pay bills and purchase online items. Nobody seems to carry cash anymore, and this is manna from heaven for cybercriminals. There are examples of cybercriminals who gain access to a bank's database and transfer just

$1 from each account. These types of transfers fly under the radar and can remain undetected for months. Huge sums have been stolen using wire transfers.

Piracy

While most of us will have been offered counterfeit DVDs and compact discs, we all know that it is illegal. Most people will recognize the crime as theft, while others will consider it their given right to take advantage of this offer of free entertainment. But what if our jobs were hijacked in the same way? What if people expected the goods and services that we supply to be free? That would be a crime, right? So why don't we pay the same respect to the jobs of people in the entertainment industry? Piracy is a crime.

Identity Theft

Most of us remember the episode of *Friends* (1994) when a fun-loving lady stole Monica Geller's identity with hilarious results. The actual crime of identity theft is possibly one of the most insidious ways that cybercriminals can affect your life. The only piece of information a criminal needs in the US is someone's social security number, and they can then steal their identity. They have access to all the documents related to that person's citizenship. They now have the power to set up a completely separate identity using the victim's name. They can acquire a driving license, open bank accounts, and run up loans. They operate on many different levels. The smallest amounts may be as low as $300, while some amounts are higher. Most Americans are aware of the possibility of identity theft and are more vigilant, which means the amounts have dropped in recent times.

Spam

If you have an email address, then you will have been sent spam of some sort. This is unsolicited emails containing advertisements or links to sites that can be at best, useless, and at worst, offensive. Spam may seem like a normal part of cyber life, but it is a crime. Worse still, it is a crime against all users of the internet. It is impossible to see how spam can be eliminated without violating the freedom of speech we all enjoy. Most of us are protected by the email providers we use, but we could all benefit from extra measures of security.

These types of crimes listed are just scratching the surface of those committed by cybercriminals. We need to know how to protect ourselves online just as much as we protect ourselves in normal life.

Protect Yourself Against Cybercriminals

The internet is not a benign place that is safe for all users. While we expect some form of protection from the social media and sites we use, we can also put some additional precautions in place. These are not just suitable for tech-savvy users but can be used by every single person who knows how to turn a computer on!

1) Use strong passwords: do you have the same password for every site you use? Is it a combination of your birthdate and a pet's name so you can remember it easier? Did you know that around 70% of adults use the same password for multiple sites? You need to change that fact! Make your passwords complex. Change them regularly. Make use of symbols, numbers, and at least ten letters that are not necessarily sequential. Use a password management app to keep a record of your new, complex passwords, and don't rely on your memory.

2) Make sure your software is updated regularly: cybercriminals are always searching for flaws in software packages. They then have a limited period of time to exploit these flaws. If you are regularly checking the package you use, you can remain one step in front of them.

3) Use a VPN: a VPN or virtual private network is a must for anyone spending time online. It protects your online privacy and makes it more difficult for hackers to trace you and your activities. You can choose a low-cost VPN from various providers to make your location and information anonymous. VPN's encrypt all the data you

send and keep you safe. VPN's are legal in most countries apart from China and Iraq, but there can be anti-privacy and censorship requirements, so make sure you check the information for your region using vpnmentor.com.

4) Back up your files regularly: use a separate storage system to store your files so you can clear them from your computer. Just like a clean house protects your physical health, a clean computer prevents online viruses and corruption.

5) Be careful what you click on: cybercriminals are waiting to lure you in with a catchy advertisement or an appealing link to a site. Never download a file from an unknown source or click on a link that isn't generated by a legitimate source.

6) Keep your financial details private: how many times have you read about bogus emails or other communications from banks asking for account details? Cybercriminals understand a legitimate-looking email will make some of us disclose our security details. Talk to your bank, and you will soon discover that they will never ask you for any details or request that you transfer money into alternate accounts.

7) Manage your social media settings: most people have at least one social media account, while many people have multiple accounts. Imagine removing the hassle of managing these accounts with just one online tool. Try CoSchedule.com for advice on how to manage your personal and business media accounts. Take Twitter, Facebook, Instagram, and Pinterest accounts and make them more secure. This type of security will help you to protect your online life and the details you reveal.

8) Understand identity theft can happen anywhere: when you leave the security of your own home, you are often putting yourself at risk from cybercriminals. When you are traveling, you may need to get information on the road. This can enable hackers to gain an insight into where you are, what hotel or resort you will be visiting, and how you are going to pay for them.

How many times have you seen friends or family using social media to advertise the fact they're going on holiday? It is normal to get excited about holidays and traveling, but declaring you are about to be away from home for two weeks is an invitation to regular thieves as well as cybercriminals. Take your VPN with you and keep the details of your trip quiet until you return home.

9) Talk to your kids about the dangers of the internet: because your kids have a clean slate regarding credit histories, they can become a target for criminals who specialize in identity theft. Explain to your children what they can and can't share on the internet. Make sure you have access to their social media accounts, and you can manage their security settings.

This is also the perfect time to tell them about the dangers that can lurk online. Nobody wants to scare their kids, but telling them to be vigilant is imperative. They need to know they can come to you if they fear they are being groomed or are facing harassment online. Bullying has reached new heights with the internet, and your kids could be at risk of online bullying and stalking.

10) Be aware of what to do if you are targeted: remember that nobody is safe online, and if you notice any abnormalities on your computer, you should report it. Inform your local police force, and they will help you decide what to do next. There are plenty of resources out there to keep you safe. If you think your financial details have been accessed, cancel all your cards immediately and get in touch with your bank.

Cybercrime is not restricted to spy novels and thrillers anymore. Online crime is fast becoming the number one way that criminals operate. The predicted cybercrime damages for 2021 is around $6 trillion just for the US. Don't become part of this statistic. Use the tips above to keep your online experience enjoyable.

Chapter 12: Protecting Yourself

Have you ever wondered why you feel strongly about some subjects, yet others pass you by? Are your opinions fueled by outside influences, or are they a true reflection of your beliefs?

We live in a democratic society, so surely, we are encouraged to think freely and form our own opinions? You would think so. But the truth is that democracy, in its purest form, is all about manipulation. We need to be told how to think and what appeals to us by people who we will never meet. If we weren't educated to think that way, our society would be in chaos.

The trouble with modern society is it seems to have taken this concept a step too far. We are subject to thinly veiled propaganda that presents itself as news. We are presented with the "facts" and information that people in powerful positions feel we should see. Misinformation and propaganda are easily spread via social media and biased online "news" websites. If it's a biased niche "news" website, whether on the left or right of the political spectrum, or a tabloid, then it is important to independently verify any "facts" and to filter out the opinions and agenda of the media organization in question. In short, we are often being treated like children, and if you look closer, you'll see when there are blatant attempts to appeal to our emotions and biases, instead of clearly presenting facts in an impartial manner.

In a nutshell, we need to stop accepting dumbed-down versions of reality and take an active part in what we absorb. Short buzz feed style headlines that grab the attention and keep us flicking from subject to subject tell us extraordinarily little, yet plant seeds of misinformation in our psyche.

Here are some ways to make sure the information you receive is relevant:

Choose Your News Source Carefully

Some news sources are more reliable than others, and some journalists are more ethical than others. This doesn't mean you can accept people's opinions or statements as facts—such as those often made in short captions on Twitter or social media—without independent verification and evidence that they are true. A lot of "false news" is spread in memes, tabloids, or on niche and highly biased "news" websites, and via social media. It is important to find reliable sources and to investigate further, using critical thinking, before believing such information. You should be presented with a balanced argument that contains any possible biases and which comes from a reliable and ethical source—not from an opinion piece, a biased headline, or statements on social media that promote conspiracy theories or can easily be proven as outright lies.

Once you start questioning the facts you are presented with; you will learn to separate propaganda from reality. There are so many sources providing you with "news" that it can feel overwhelming.

Reliable Sources That Produce Quality Journalism

1) *The Wall Street Journal*: when you choose to read the WSJ, you know what to expect. The publication produces highly accurate articles with a conservative bias. Once you accept this, you can rely on it to supply you with information that has come from a trusted source.

2) *The BBC*: this well-known British institution is respected across the globe for its accurate content and lack of bias. When the BBC reports on political stories, it focuses on what politicians have said and little else. It doesn't use its own views to influence viewers, which is something that can't be said about most US news networks. The BBC's commentary is generally factual and trustworthy.

3) *The Economist*: this publication has been around for over 150 years and has a liberal stance about most stories. It is a trustworthy source of news with clear facts. *The Economist* publishes opinion pieces as well as straightforward news stories. However, it clearly states that opinion pieces are exactly that, the journalist is stating their personal opinion and trying to persuade us to agree. *The Economist* is a serious source of intelligent and trustworthy news and is considered the most trusted news source in the US.

Read More

While the news is important, it should be balanced out with other reading matter. Try nonfiction books to widen your understanding of the world and enjoy a classic piece of fiction instead of turning on the television. Read widely about history, theology, or scientific subjects. The mind is capable of great things if only you give it some information to work with.

Don't Take Sides in Politics

You can only get a balanced view of a subject by considering all sides. You will have a bias; we all do, but if you only listen to people who have the same views as you, how will you form a balanced opinion? Try being a devil's advocate and read literature as if you were a supporter of the opposing party. If you can cast your affiliations to one side, you will become a more informed voter who can take part in political debates with confidence.

Become a Clear Thinker

Now you have reliable sources for your news; it's time to address how you think about other aspects of your life. Are you swept up by popular opinions and find yourself agreeing with statements just to fit in? That is not healthy, you are an individual, and it's time you asserted yourself as the free-thinking version of yourself.

Ways to Clear Your Mind and Think for Yourself

Create a Healthy Mind Space

Have you always got your mind on your social media, or do you constantly check emails and your phone for messages? Remember the good old days when we didn't feel the need to connect to everyone 24/7? Maybe you don't; maybe you are too young to remember those bygone days when we could just turn off for an hour and give our brains a rest. If that is the case, it may be more difficult for you to imagine an hour a day without stimuli from your electronic devices.

However, giving your brain a chance to breathe will be an eye-opener for everyone. We are bombarded with requests, nuggets of information, or we feel compelled to fill every minute with tasks. What happened to alone time? Why do we feel that time spent alone isn't relevant?

Call it meditation, call it recouping your mental ground, call it "me time." Whatever you call it, just do it. That means no phone, no laptop, no television, no book, and even no radio or music. You are about to meet your brain and have a meaningful chat. Enjoy!

Refuse to Be Pushed into Anything

We are surrounded by click-bait forms of media and information. It requires instant decisions, and uninformed replies. You may be used to seeing a post online and replying in seconds. This is a form of addiction and must be stopped. The world will not implode if you fail to comment on what your friend thinks about a cute puppy post.

Ask questions about what you see. Is it relevant to your life, and will you benefit from any aspect of it? If the answer is no, then ignore it. Don't be a sheep, don't follow popular opinion just to fit in. Be the person who questions the preconceived notions we are all subject to.

Give Yourself Time to Consider All Options

If you need more time to consider your decisions, then say so. Be firm and tell the world you are not going to be pushed around. It may seem like an alien concept the first couple of times you try it, but as your confidence grows, so will your resolve.

Learn from Mistakes

We all make them; we all see others make them. Mistakes, errors, flaws, and gaffes are all part of human life. Why then are we made to feel like a failure whenever we make them? Hold your hands up, admit you were wrong, and encourage yourself to learn from mistakes. Other people will see you are willing to admit when you are wrong and respect you for it.

How to Avoid Being Manipulated in Relationships

We have discussed how psychological warfare can affect relationships and lead to one partner being the manipulator. If you feel the situation is completely out of control, then you must end it. But if there is a chance to make something happen to improve the relationship, then you should try.

1) Ask your partner something fresh and exciting: if you have been together for some time, it could be that communication has become a habit. "How was your day?" and "What happened at work?" are boring when asked daily. Try making an effort and asking something you really want to know. Try questions like: "What was the best memory of your childhood?" or "Have you ever dreamed of traveling in space, and what do you think it would be like?" When you put in extra effort to create a meaningful conversation, you show your partner another side to you. You want to know more about them because you love them.

2) Make time for them: both of you should be able to have independent activities, and this is important. However, sometimes we can be inflexible when tweaking our schedules in case it seems like we are showing weakness. Try compromising. Maybe you could drop that spin class or gym session to go to that movie premiere they want to attend. You shouldn't have to make sacrifices, but compromises are fine.

3) Let go of the past: if you have had concerns about past behavior, then you need to draw a line under it and move on. By agreeing to try again, you are saying you forgive them. This means you can't let past issues affect your future.

4) Remember the small things: sometimes, we worry too much about grand gestures and overblown displays of affection. Small details can be just as important. For instance, if your partner mentions they need to have an important meeting with a client next week, then make a note of the day they are meeting. When your partner arrives home that evening bring up the subject. They will be pleased you remembered, and it will show you care.

5) Show affection: are you guilty of complacency in your relationship? Maybe you both are, and it can seem stale. Bring back the romance and show your partner some affection. Grab their hand when out shopping or surprise them with a romantic night in! Flowers and candy may seem like kids' stuff, but they work!

Every relationship is different, and none are perfect no matter what you are told. Quality relationships are what we all crave, but sometimes we must put the effort in. If you feel the relationship is worth saving, you will know the best ways to make sure that happens.

How to Avoid Manipulation in General

First, you must realize that everybody can be a jerk now and then, but some people seem incapable of being anything else. Toxic people are often incapable of change, so they should be avoided. If you know that certain people are hell-bent on making you feel miserable, why are you still in contact with them?

Get rid of people who are Dr Jekyll and Mr Hyde type personalities. We are all prone to mood swings, but when someone is completely lovely to you one day and then prickly or bad-tempered the next day, they could have a toxic personality. If they refuse to answer your calls or disappear from your life for days on end with no apparent reason, then they are messing with your emotions. This type of manipulation is not acceptable, and they should be cut from your life.

Be Aware of Your Own Feelings

When we experience manipulation or emotional abuse, we are often left with feelings that are hard to define. We worry too much about what the other person is feeling and what we have done to upset them. Take the time to reflect on your own feelings for a change. Are you experiencing guilt or shame about your actions? Why should you feel bad about someone else's behavior?

The truth is that reasonable, balanced, emotionally stable people often care more about being decent to others than they do about their feelings. Stop doing that and listen to the alarm bells ringing in your head. You have no reason to be feeling shame or guilt. Start feeling angry about how you have been treated and realize you have done nothing wrong.

Become a Good Listener

There is a distinct difference between someone trying to manipulate you and someone who is trying to get you to see their point of view. We can be too defensive if we have experienced manipulation in the past. Open your ears and try to understand what the other person is trying to tell you. If they are prone to using generalizations and blanket statements that are designed to squash your views, then call them out on it.

Narcissists don't want to hear your nuances, and they will refuse to acknowledge them. If all you can hear is black and white illogical terms, then walk away. You should state the reason for your departure. Tell them your time is too precious to listen to their "broken record" style of rhetoric.

Avoid Triangulation

Do you have a certain friend who will repeatedly tell you what other people are saying about you? They will tell you it's for your own good and you need to know the truth about how people see you. They love to report back falsehoods about what third parties are saying. This is one way that manipulators try and draw you in. They present themselves as the only trustworthy person in your life.

This method is known as "triangulation" and should be avoided at all costs. You should realize that the third party in the drama is just as much a victim as yourself. Try reversing the situation and join forces with the third party to turn the tables on the manipulating party.

Improve Your Frame Control

What is your "frame control?" Put simply; it is how you react to an interaction. Life is full of interactions, and how you view them is how you control your frame. They can be affected by time, location, intent, and natural flow. A strong frame requires a strong intention. You should know your mind and demonstrate to others that you are not easily swayed.

For instance, take the example of a salesman and customer. The customer has the intention of finding out a price without buying a product as he wants to explore other options. The salesman has the frame of selling the customer something no matter what. The individual with the strongest frame control will achieve their objective.

Frame Strengthening Exercises

If you feel your frame may be susceptible and needs work, then try these frame strengthening exercises. Just like regular muscles, your mind needs a workout every now and then.

1) Stick to a list: if you find the lure of the supermarket too difficult to ignore, try this simple task. Make a list and don't buy anything else. If you are determined to eat healthily, you can be distracted by a well-placed bag of chips! Use frame control to stick to essentials.

2) Make someone smile every day: when you have a strong frame, people want to be with you. If you can make people smile with your personality, you are halfway there. Nobody is suggesting you turn into a standup comedian but try being amusing. Consider the goal of making one person per day smile.

3) Go to sleep on time: have you ever outframed yourself at bedtime? You know you have a busy day tomorrow, and you should be asleep by 11 pm, but it's way past midnight, and you're still giving yourself ten more minutes before you go to bed. Decide on your bedtime and stick to it.

4) Join an acting class: if you want to become a force of nature, then take lessons from professionals! An acting class will help you to project your voice, use your mannerisms to get your meaning across and hold a strong frame. Acting is all about becoming a different person for a fixed time. If you want to be a believable consummate actor, then take a class.

5) Have life goals: people with strong frames tend to have set goals in life. Those with weaker frames will tend to drift. If you have well-defined goals in life, you can discard trivialities. Become more focused and believe you can achieve whatever you set out to do. Set goals in career, relationship, health, and spiritual matters to become a well-rounded individual with an awesome frame.

The importance of your frame can't be stressed enough. If you have a confident, optimistic frame of mind, you will recognize potential psychological attacks. You will also learn how to analyze what others are saying to you and discard trivial matters.

The bottom line is that we are all subject to PSYOPS every day. You will know what your weaknesses are and how to deal with them.

There is no one quick fix to rid your life of toxic people, but a combination of methods will help you to live a healthier and happier life.

Conclusion

Thank you for reading *Psychological Warfare: The Ultimate Guide to Understanding Human Behavior, Brainwashing, Propaganda, Deception, Negotiation, Dark Psychology, and Manipulation.* Now you know the dangers of psychological warfare and the prevalence of it in society. Knowledge is power, and knowing how to deal with people can also be empowering.

Unless you plan on living in a cave for the rest of your life, you will have social interactions, and knowing how to navigate them is a key ingredient for success. You are also now better equipped to decipher between what is real and what is false news and to recognize the use of propaganda. Good luck with your newfound knowledge—use it well!

Here's another book by Neil Morton that you might like

References

http://www.thoughtco.com

http://www.sciencedaily.com

http://www.scientificamerican.com

http://www.theconversation.com

http://www.psychologytoday.com

http://psychcentral.com

http://www.time.com

http://www.bustle.com

http://www.rewire.org

http://www.historians.org

https://exploringyourmind.com

http://www.theverge.com

http://www.cracked.com

http://interestingengineering.com

http://www.howstuffworks.com

http://www.iapm.net

http://www.theplaidzebra.com

http://www.aconsciousrethink.com

http://www.parcast.com

http://www.everygirl.com

http://www.lifehacker.com

CPSIA information can be obtained
at www.ICGtesting.com
Printed in the USA
BVHW041204041120
592495BV00007BA/302